RIDING ON THE
POWER OF OTHERS

-A Horsewoman's Path to Unconditional Love-

REN HURST

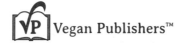 Vegan Publishers™

Some names have been changed in this book
to protect the privacy of the individuals involved.

Published by:
Vegan Publishers, Danvers, MA, www.veganpublishers.com

Cover and text design: Nicola May Design
Photograpy: Brandy Setzer and Ren Hurst

❂ Printed in the United States of America on 100% recycled paper

ISBN 978-1-940184-11-1

*For **Annie***

And in loving memory of
Philippe Bertaud,
*who eternally touched my soul and reminded me
that a life without passion and joy is no life at all.*

Contents

Foreword

There is something so wonderful about reading a good book. I just love being drawn into a story, experiencing it as if I am one of the characters, and living the story as if the character's journey was my own. That's exactly what happened for me when I read *Riding on the Power of Others*. I couldn't put it down.

I also happened to be fortunate enough to watch much of the wonderful transformation that took place in the author's life as she wrote this book. I can tell you that throughout the process, her hunger to make a difference in the lives of others has only expanded as her clarity of purpose has become more focused. Though she and I had met just a few months prior, I sensed that knowing Ren would positively affect my life. Reading her manuscript simply deepened that feeling. I believe you will find it affects your life in a similar way.

Some of my favorite books are written like this one. Personal-growth stories told by people who have the willingness and courage to openly change their lives, even when doing so might bring about some unpleasant attention. I love reading authors who yearn to become grander versions of themselves, regardless of any "sticks and stones" moments they may endure. Any brief discomfort that might be caused by the negative opinions of others is preferable to missing the opportunity brought about by real change. Still, each of us must choose to take that kind of risk, and we either make the change or not. Both choices have predictable outcomes—choose wisely.

Ren recognized and approached her learned beliefs with compassion and a willingness to consider other points of view.

She realized, as all critical thinkers do, that it isn't about whether others are "right" or "wrong," but rather about finding their truth. Just as it takes courage to change in life, it takes guts to read a book like this. This book may challenge the very fabric of some of your firmly held beliefs.

Besides examining her thinking, Ren also began to trust and follow her intuition and insights into new possibilities for her life, even when to do so would challenge everything she had held sacred before. I'm not suggesting that this was or is an easy process (it clearly wasn't for Ren, as you will discover). Yet it's these very insights and this willingness to question everything we think we know that kick open the door barring us from a grander way of living. As our paradigm changes, many of the thinking patterns that we are accustomed to simply no longer work. No matter how long a particular belief has been held by humanity, when the time of change has come, resistance is futile. Having the courage to go to the edge and expand our beliefs—or letting them go altogether—is what Ren's story is all about.

You may find an opportunity to change presented within these pages. Your invitation is to not only recognize your own learned beliefs, but whether or not what you have learned represents you on this day. If it doesn't, then let the new learning begin.

The intention of the author was not to make anyone feel "wrong" for how they have chosen to live their life. Rather, she encourages us to explore what life would be like if we embraced change, continued to explore answers to larger questions, and sought a grander way to be and become, not only with ourselves but with every living creature we are connected to here on Earth.

Please remember as you read this book, or move through any process in life, to look through the eyes of love and compassion. Be willing to let go of judgment, which leads to condemnation and serves no one. The outcome of judgment is predictable, painful, and pointless. Simply choose love again and again. This is the highest choice any being can make.

If I were to sum up this book with one quote it would be the following, attributed to Jimi Hendrix: "When the power of love overcomes the love of power, the world will know peace." Ren invites us to embrace the power of love rather than the love of power. Her relationship with horses showed her the true healing power and potential of unconditional love. Many of those horses now assist in her work of healing not only other horses, but humans, too.

One of my favorite things to do now is spend the day at Ren's sanctuary. The unconditional love found there lights me up. I appreciate it all so much more now that I have read her book and understand her journey to find the love that was within her all along.

Now it's your turn. I hope reading her book will touch you as deeply as it has me.

With love,

JR Westen, D.D., C.A.d.

J.R. Westen is a counselor and Executive Director for the Conversations with God Foundation in Ashland, Oregon. He serves on the Board of Trustees for the New World Sanctuary Foundation.

In Gratitude

Though a lifetime of experience was necessary beforehand, this book was written in its entirety and picked up by a publisher in less than 90 days' time. When such things occur in my life, I have absolutely no doubt that I had very little to do with any of it. This may be my personal story, but the message is for all of us, and it is with deepest gratitude that I thank the horses most especially – for sacrificing happiness, comfort, and even their lives for old pleasures and for what I now hope will become our evolution.

This story would not be possible without the lessons from my childhood or the unwavering support of my family. Even when they question my sanity, not a one has ever tried to keep me from pursuing my dreams, and I thank them endlessly for that and for making me the strong, resilient woman I am today. For all the friends and former clients back home in Texas that put up with an enormous amount of uncomfortable change, this thanks extends to you as well.

Writing this book, especially with how much I procrastinated and how long I put it off, was an overwhelming endeavor at times. I want to extend a huge thank you to Sas Petherick, who coached me through, beginning to end; and to Brenda Peck and Diane "Little Saturn Big Tree" Saturnino, who read every word along the way and provided immediate support and feedback from their huge, unconditional hearts; and to Jackie Scott, who was an absolute angel and friend during a time when I needed it the most.

I am blown away at how quick and easy the process of writing a book and being published can be when everything is in alignment. It is with great humility and appreciation that I thank the entire team at Vegan Publishers for their interest in my story and for allowing me to be a voice for horses on such a huge scale. This is a real dream come true, and you made it completely stress free. To everyone who provided such valuable and generous feedback along the way, thank you. A very special thank you to JR Westen for providing the foreword to this book, for inspiring my writing to truly be unleashed, and for believing in me.

To all those past and present who took the time to educate, share with, and expand me in so many ways concerning horse care – thank you. I am so grateful for each person I have met on this path and for what they added to this amazing journey and my own personal growth.

To Alexander and Lydia Nevzorov – I am forever thankful for your influence on me and the horses I love. Your unyielding commitment to your truth has had such an impact on the way the world views horses and the horse-human relationship. I will always stand up strong for the Horse Revolution with great respect for all the work you have done. This thank you must also include my dear friend, Stormy May, for introducing me to the Nevzorovs through her amazing documentary, "The Path of The Horse." Thank you all for leading the way.

Nothing in my life has had a greater positive influence on me than my time at High Hope Ranch and all the fostering connections developed there. Her sacred ground, the safety in which I was taught, and the comfort of knowing her as home expanded me in ways I never imagined and at a pace some would call remarkable. To Krystyna, Chandler, and Dharma – you changed my life and inspired all that I am and will become. I love you and hold you in deepest gratitude.

And finally, to the woman who opened my heart to the experience of unconditional love – my first true partner in life, my very best friend, Brandy Setzer. I have only found me because of you. You have graced me with the truest kind of love between two people, the most intimate of friendships, and an allowing that has given me courage beyond all limitations. Without your unwavering support, none of it would be possible. Thank you for loving me for exactly who I am, even when it isn't easy. I will spend eternity loving you exactly the same way.

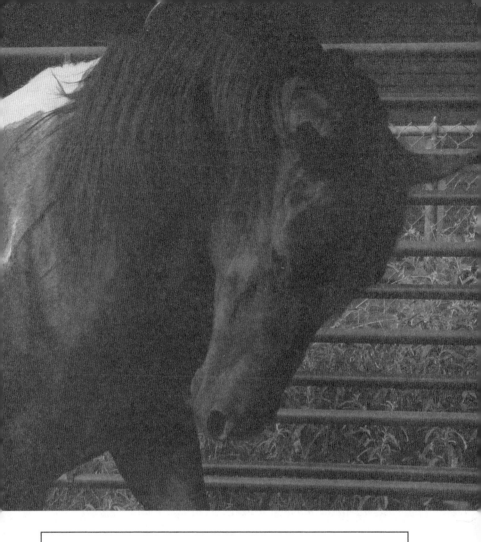

ONE

-Dreaming in Black & White-

"A horse is the projection of peoples' dreams about themselves—strong, powerful, beautiful—and it has the capability of giving us escape from our mundane existence."
~ Pam Brown

{His mere presence could stop time. As he stepped forward out of the darkness, the strength and power of his sheer essence hit me in waves. Every hair on my body stood on end. My heart was pounding. All the voices disappeared and were replaced with the kind of focus that comes instantly when survival is at stake. Being with him was like living in slow motion. The way the dirt left the ground with each foot fall. The way his coat shimmered in the faintest light. The way he proudly threw his mane and tossed his head, as if nothing in this life could present an obstacle he wasn't ready to face with fierce courage. He was a stallion. Proud and brave, he arched his neck and flared his nostrils as he moved toward me with determination. He was challenging me. I mirrored back his language, and with my heartbeat in my throat, I accepted his invitation...

The dream ended with my heart racing. It is rare that I receive clear messages while I'm sleeping, but I was just sure that this dream was a promise to deliver something I desperately wanted – a horse that would make headlines with me in the evolution of horsemanship. I was ready to take my skill and experience as a horse trainer to the level I had always imagined I would reach for, and I just had a feeling it would be a black and white stallion, out of my mare, to get me there. I had been stud shopping for weeks for the perfect horse to breed to my mare, Velvet. I had finally settled on a stunning black and white National Show Horse, a flashy pinto cross between an Arabian and a Saddlebred, of 17.2 hands high. I imagined my dream was a glimpse of the colt in my future and a sure sign that Velvet would indeed deliver a colt to me, but I wasn't prepared for what was really in store.

Still a bit shaken with eyes not fully awake, I sat down at my computer to check the morning's e-mails. The first message in the inbox was from one of my hoof care clients, and there was an attachment. It was a photo of a black and white stallion, and he was in dire need of my help. I had no way of understanding it at the time, but the Death Card had just been played in my favor. (To be cont. in Chapter 13)}

+++++++++++++

My first horse was a semi-surprise from my mom on my 12th birthday. I walked outside the front door of our very residential neighborhood home to find a young, sorrel filly, saddled and tied to the tree in our front yard by the reins.

Katy Bug was three years old, a race-bred quarter horse filly, and probably the worst decision anyone could have ever made as a first horse for an inexperienced young girl. My only mentors in horsemanship knew absolutely nothing about horses, despite their own claims, so it was an interesting partnership for a while, for sure. Katy had champion race horses all over her registration papers, and to this day, I still do not understand or even want to know how my mom was able to purchase her for me. I knew she was worth a lot of money in the right hands, and for the time being, I was just happy she landed in the wrong ones.

I grew up in a struggling, middle-class family. I was a smart kid, and I excelled easily at academics. I was also good at sports and music, but I lacked the confidence to pursue either anywhere close to the reaches of my potential. Love in our home looked like all sorts of crazy. There were kind words and touching, but they were often overshadowed by a much darker and painful reality. However, there were always animals, and they were my source of sanity for as long as I can remember. I studied animals endlessly and could tell you any dog's breed as well as recite the family, genus, and species of most mammals around the globe. Wolves and big cats were my favorite, and I had big dreams of becoming a biologist and wildlife rehabilitator, living out in the wild, far away from the only animals I couldn't stand—humans. There was a vast array of mild abuses throughout my childhood involving violence, sexual misconduct, and a nasty divorce and custody battle that included a short stint in foster care, to name a few. I was a spoiled brat with little structure, and I rarely felt safe, calm, or heard. I lived with my mother and stepfather until the age of 15, only seeing my father every other weekend, if that. All three of my parents did the absolute best they knew how to do, and as I grew older and looked into each of their own histories and upbringings, I learned to be grateful for my own experiences, despite how challenging they were. Up until that point, though, I was just one pissed-off girl at war with the world around me.

By age five, I had been molested and placed in sexual situations with other children by older children whom I trusted. I had no idea I was being abused, and I continued the behavior for years. This led to many, many years of an unhealthy relationship with and understanding of sex and intimacy, as well as deep guilt and shame that followed me into adulthood. It also resulted in my being non-violently raped at the age of fourteen.

I don't remember a time in my childhood where fighting wasn't the go-to solution to any problem. Verbally or physically, by observing those around me, that is how I was taught to solve my issues. The police were regular visitors to our home for domestic disputes, and I had seen a gun drawn and pointed at someone in defense more than once. I had been taught to use one myself and was quite comfortable with them despite having been accidentally shot in the face by my older brother when I was five years old, while lying on the couch at my grandmother's, watching My Little Pony on television. I was rushed into emergency surgery to remove the little bullet from where it lodged below my jaw, and I still remember quite well the way the metal surgical tools clanked against my tiny skull. The doctor told us that if the bullet had entered even one inch higher, I could have been killed. It was the first of many scars to come.

Hospitals were a familiar place. I was in and out of them all the time, just like my mother, for various illnesses or surgery. The two times I ever found the courage to try out for sports, I broke my arm the same day. The first time was at age ten—a complex multiple fracture of my right arm the day I was to sign up for the public soccer league. The second time was in seventh grade when I tried out for the basketball team. I showed up the day after tryouts, with a red cast halfway up my forearm, just to learn that I had made A-team point guard....the most coveted spot on the best team. I spent the season mostly on the bench, and my confidence on the court plummeted. To make matters worse, soon after, I watched my mother die in front of me at home following a grand mal seizure. I called 911, and the paramedics were able to revive her, but not until after the lack of oxygen had affected her speech and cognition. She eventually fully recovered, but it was a very challenging time in my life, and I remember being very confused about a lot of things. For one, the paramedic team seemed annoyed, at best, to be in our home that day, and I had several adults, including my basketball coach, approach me and ask if I would like to come live with them for a while. I had no idea at the time why anyone would ask such things, and it scared me.

By age 13, I was out of control, and my parents could barely handle me. I did what I wanted, with whomever I wanted, and I used manipulation and intimidation to get my way. I had learned a great deal about manipulation from the adults in my life and how they often played me against each other in their personal disputes. My mother's solution was pretty much to bend to my every whim. I had zero respect for her or my stepfather, and if threats were made, I would make my own threats in return. If physical violence was suggested or directed at me, I tensed up and told them to bring it on. Depression and anger became all too familiar, and horses became my drug of choice for relief. I was very fortunate to be surrounded by good friends and their families, mostly because my ease at academic excellence put me in a good circle of influence, even if it was small.

The sad stories and challenges of my childhood are not what this book is about, but I feel it important to give you a glimpse into my early development in order for an understanding to take place in regard to my journey with horses and where I started. You see, I didn't dream of caring for and falling in love with beautiful horses the way a lot of young girls do. I just saw a way to be swiftly carried away from the often-horrendous circumstances of my life.

If you know anything at all about horses, you might know that a three-year-old, green broke filly and a 12-year-old, pissed-off, human girl aren't exactly a good match for a first-horse combination. I had no idea how to get Katy Bug to listen to me, and I wasn't all that interested in listening to her. I just wanted to ride. I wanted to escape the hand I had been dealt and run as fast on those race-bred legs as they could carry me. Only problem was, I couldn't get her to go hardly anywhere that I wanted to go, much less at the speed I requested....or demanded. It was a very frustrating time. I had my horse, finally, but I couldn't do much with her, and I had little help. My brilliant solution was to fill a bucket full of sweet feed in the barn, then walk Katy to the farthest end of the property we leased for her. At that point, I would hop on, hit her butt with a crop, and hold on for dear life with tears streaming out of my eyes from the speed and impact of the air hitting my face. She was so fast. This had to be what freedom felt like, and I was instantly addicted.

That was pretty much my riding life for a while, mixed with many other failed attempts at trying to do things in a way that made more sense. Believe it or not, Katy did begin listening to me a bit more throughout all of this, and even more unbelievable—that horse never once hurt me. I was fearless outside of anger for the first time in my life. I could have been killed a hundred times over with all the crazy stunts I pulled to get to feel the wind on my face, but she took care of me every step of the way, and I somehow knew I did not have to be afraid of her. I must have hurt her in more ways than I will ever care to remember considering how very little I knew back then, but the love I felt for her and what we did together must have meant something to her-something that allowed her to take care of me despite my very deep ignorance and how much physical pain she must have endured for me. Love always prevails over pain, even if the love is buried very deep under bullshit.

TWO

-Fancy My Pain-

"Look back at our struggle for freedom,
Trace our present day's strength to its source;
And you'll find that man's pathway to glory
Is strewn with the bones of the horse."
~ Author Unknown

{I sat there, bruised and cut up, and the tears streamed from my eyes. I thought you cared about me, but just like everyone else, when it came to what you needed, I was going to be left on my ass, in the dirt. I hated this life. It was so deeply unfair. I remembered back in sixth grade playing a palm reading game with a few other kids. The game was supposed to determine the age in which you would die. My palm said I would die at the age of 21. I remember thinking, "Thank God, at least I don't have to keep this up for too much longer." Then I heard your hooves pounding towards me, your frantic whinny calling out. I held my breath and the tears stopped. You were running back to me, looking around frantically. Could it be?

Did you really just leave your bucket of feed and your companion at the barn to come back and look for me? It's true, you hadn't really dumped me at all; I had just miscalculated the speed and distance at which to jump, and I couldn't hold on fast enough. It was so much easier to blame you, though. But you came back seeming desperate and concerned.

No, I can't deal with this. I felt a burning sensation in my chest. It still hurt too much to stand up, so I picked up several rocks around me. I began throwing them at you and screaming at you to go away and leave me alone, the tears again streaming down my red, hot cheeks. You wouldn't leave, Fancy.. You paced and zigzagged around me, urging me to get back on my feet. I refused. You waited.

I couldn't believe you had come back, and I also couldn't accept it. Yet, you had given me a glimpse of what horses are capable of, and it wasn't something I could forget. The pain and anger inside me were too much to allow it to reach me, though, and instead, I decided right then that it would be safer to not experience such things. I stood up, and we walked back to the barn in silence, side by side but no interaction between us. Love wasn't something I was ready to receive. It was just too much.}

+++++++++++++

Eventually, my frustration with trying to get Katy to listen to me really set in, and I wanted more. I was bored, and I wanted to be able to make decisions from the back of my horse. I also wanted to be able to ride with someone else, and I had no friends with horses, so I wanted another horse that my friends could ride. I convinced my mom that I needed another horse, so along came Fancy. Fancy would have been the perfect first horse for a girl like me. She was small, just around 13 hands high; around seven years old; and was previously trained by a girl not much older than I was. The combination of me and Fancy was amazing. She tried anything I asked, and without knowing anything about horse training as a concept, I was able to teach her to jump and carry me bareback absolutely anywhere I wished to go. I was feeling confident outside of my comfort zone for the first time, and the whistles I got from little boys riding their bikes as I road bareback on my pony down old country roads didn't hurt me in the self-esteem department either. Unfortunately, that kind of attention does not lead to true confidence, but rather to a much darker path indeed, especially for a kid like me.

I was tough. I'd fight boys until they had bloody noses. I played football as well as any boy I knew. I was hanging out with boys much older than I was and learning things I did not need to know at such a young age. I was still so angry, and at this point, the horses were still an outlet of love, as I knew it; of freedom; and of escape. To me, love was feeling good in the presence of another, and that was about as far as my understanding could reach. As good as Fancy was to me, there was still one craving I could not get her to satisfy—running full speed and feeling the wind try to rip me off her back. She was not nearly as fast as Katy Bug, but food—especially food laden with sweet molasses—is a very strong motivational force for a horse. I was still using that technique to get my adrenaline fix; however, with Fancy, it was even more bold and daring. The girls had worn a specific path from the corner of the property where I used to take

Katy for our crazy joy rides. There was a big rock I could stand on right next to the path, and when I whistled, the girls would come galloping up the path to the barn to get their food. As they would run by, I would leap into the air and land on Fancy's back, giggling like a wild thing all the way to the barn. What a rush!

One day—my plan didn't work out so well. I whistled, the horses ran, I leapt—and the horses kept running while I landed hard and ass first onto the dirt and rocks below. I sat on the ground, bawling—not because of the pain, though it did hurt, but because my pride was seriously bruised, and as usual, I was pissed off. The girls were long gone, probably at the barn stuffing their faces with sugar. As tears rolled down my cheeks and my face burned in frustration, I heard a very unfamiliar sound. It was whinnying, but it was stressed, as if something were very wrong. Suddenly, Fancy came tearing back down the path, anxiously searching for something and pacing and running all over the place. Then she spotted me and screamed louder, running right for me. I instantly realized she had come back for me. I almost felt the love of that horse, realizing she had left her equine companion and her main motivation in life, her food, to come back for me—almost felt it. Sobbing heavily, I picked up rocks and threw them at her and yelled at her to go away. She refused. She would not leave me, knowing full well Katy was probably at the barn devouring both of their feed buckets. I eventually stood up and stomped back to the barn, more angry at the world than maybe ever before, not realizing that I had just been given my first real glimpse of unconditional love—and I couldn't even allow myself to feel it.

Our relationship was never the same. My life had become very chaotic at home. What Fancy had shown me was too painful to deal with, and on top of that, I had a human boyfriend to devote my attention to. My walls were up, and they weren't coming down any time soon. At this age, money was becoming something seemingly very important in life, and I realized that because of my accomplishments with Fancy, she was worth a great deal more than what we had paid for her. I decided to try to sell her. I listed her online and very quickly had a buyer interested from North Carolina. It all happened so quickly. I was so proud of myself for conducting such a large business deal, online even, and making a huge chunk of money for someone my age. The only problem was—the woman who purchased Fancy e-mailed me a few days after the shipper had dropped her off in North Carolina, and she was furious, demanding a refund. She claimed that Fancy was closer to 30 years old (absolutely not true) and that she was a cribber and had already destroyed her new barn. I didn't really know what that meant, especially since we had her in an open pasture and hadn't noticed any problems or anything to be concerned about with her. She also said she was sick, which must have happened on the journey to her new destination, if it were true at all. I tried to rectify the situation as best as my young mind could at the time, but I had already spent the money on my first vehicle. When I told the woman my age (she had engaged in business, online, buying a horse unseen, with a 15-year-old from another state), she flipped. I received an e-mail the next day telling me Alpo was on their way to pick up this horrible creature I had sold her, and I never heard from the woman again. Something broke inside of me, but the wall I had already built somehow just got taller and thicker and stronger than ever. I pushed the pain way down deep and made an unconscious decision that horses were business, not personal, and the stage was set for the journey you are about to read. I looked up Fancy's registration information years later—and she was never transferred out of my name.

THREE

-Kick Until You Win-

"One reason why birds and horses are happy is because they are not trying to impress other birds and horses."
~ Dale Carnegie

{I loved you in the dark of night, when critical eyes couldn't see. After hours, when work was done and stars twinkled above, I'd climb onto your bare back from the fence rail while you ate your hay, and I'd turn around backwards so that my feet could cross over your sweat-soaked withers and my head could rest on your soft, smooth rump. More often than not, I'd fall fast asleep within minutes.

I never told anyone, but these were my favorite times with you. Actually, any time we were alone, I was happy to be with you; but as I grew and learned, riding was never my favorite part. Something was tugging at my heart, something beyond my understanding and not supported by the voices around me. No one spoke of this whisper that I couldn't make out, and it remained unheard, though I felt it with you.

Years later, I learned a little more, and I realized how I had failed you. I was not strong enough to face it. I was not strong enough to be better for you or to wrap my arms around you and tell you how much I had grown to love you and how you saved my life. So I did the best thing I knew how to do at the time. I sold you to another little girl who I knew would love you, and I tried my best to pass on everything I had learned, so that she could be better for you than I was. I failed you in every way, and I didn't know that for a very long time. I'm so sorry, Katy Bug. I never allowed another red horse into my heart, and you're the reason why.}

+++++++++++++

Not long after Fancy was gone, my life took a major turn. At the age of 15, I very suddenly moved in with my father and left my mother's world behind. For a little while, that meant leaving Katy Bug behind as well. I was introduced to the world of structure, responsibility, and financial stability for the first time at home. I also got a reality check with strict rules and responsibilities. My father was good to me, but he was also very hard on me, and we argued about damn near everything.

I was desperate to have my horse back. As much as I loved and respected my father, this much time together was new territory, and none of it was easy. I needed to be able to ride and be who I was in order to survive his world of rules and achievement. As fate would have it, he was seriously dating a woman at the time whose parents had been professional horse trainers. One was a barrel racer, and the other was a champion roper. I was ecstatic. They had a little ranch about a half hour from our house where I could keep Katy and get my very first formal riding instruction; and by this time I had my driver's license, so it was perfect.

I loved the structure of their place. It was immaculate. Everything had a place. There were many rules and new responsibilities for me to learn. They were hesitant to take me and my now seven-year-old mare on for our first real learning as partners. It was widely accepted at that time that older horses couldn't be taught anything, especially mares. That was just one of many, many concepts horses would prove to me over the years to be completely false. As they tested Katy out to see how workable she might be, they were very impressed with her intellect and ability to pick up new training, and so we began.

They taught me how to saddle her correctly, how to clean out her hooves, and how to get her into a wash stall for a bath. They had a beautiful arena, and my first two major lessons were how to lunge her from the ground and then how to sit a trot on her back. I hated—and I mean absolutely hated—watching them prepare her for these tasks. She was a spirited horse, and I sat back and remained quiet while they used a stud chain to teach her to stay in the circle of her lunge line. Then they handed the rope to me and taught me how to pop it just right so that the chain would rap against her nose when she disobeyed; and while part of me died each time—there was a darker part that enjoyed it. Somehow, if felt horrible to harm someone I loved or to watch her being harmed, and at the same time, it felt good to give the pain inside of me an outlet. Even better was that my outlet came with approval from my elders. I enjoyed making Katy listen to me for once, and all it took was a little pop of a chain across her nose to get her to do what I wanted her to do.

As my father's relationship grew with this couple's daughter, and mine with all of them, I grew to respect these people and blindly trust their guidance. Who was I to question these things? I didn't know anything about horses and neither did my family, and these were award-winning champion horse trainers who were very well respected and acknowledged for their horsemanship throughout the community. I will never forget, though, the day that the man prepared Katy for me to be able to start serious arena work. She had no formal training after we initially purchased her. If anything, I had made her worse by the methods I had used to get to "fly without wings." She was obstinate when that kind of structure was forced upon her (like someone else I knew), and he came down on her like a mighty hammer. I watched her run for the arena wall, and I saw as he took the split leather reins and literally beat her in the face with them until she submitted and did what was asked. I saw her eyes roll back. I saw the fear. I saw part of her break. I saw the anger in his eyes when it happened. However, now I had a horse I could ride in a way that meant I might have a future with horses that looked like ribbons, a career, and real accomplishments. I also had an external outlet for the internal pain I felt. Better yet, it was not only condoned for me to take it out on her when she disobeyed—it was celebrated.

I drove out there for my lessons every day after school. Once they had taught me the techniques to properly sit my trot, tip Katy's nose into the middle of the arena to prepare for showing and proper turns, and gently lay my rein against the opposite side of her neck to push her into the turns, I was left on my own to show up, do the work, and prepare my horse for my first show. The only problem was that this was no longer fun for me—or Katy. Now, it felt like work. The freedom, the joy, the excitement of what might happen next was all gone. I was so incredibly grateful to them for showing me how to tack her up on my own and take care of her needs and especially for how to ride properly and move with her body so that we felt like one. That was a great gift indeed, but I was still a broken kid. Freedom and escape from my thoughts were what I was after.

I started showing up with a novel. I would go through the motions, walk Katy into the arena, climb on board, and break open my book across the saddle horn. I was pretty skilled at controlling her by now, so we'd just trot along our designated route, and I would read and sing to her and enjoy our lesson. Until, that is, they caught on to what I was doing. I couldn't quite understand it, but everyone was disappointed in me. I had used all of their valuable time and effort just to be lazy, or so it was expressed. To make it worse, one day when I was really craving the wind in my face, I walked Katy to the far end of the arena and pointed her toward the gate—then I climbed on board and let her rip. We barreled for the gate at lightning speed, and it was the first time that same smile had come across my face since all of our adventures tearing across the old pasture to the bucket full of feed at the barn. To my dismay, everyone came running wild-eyed and yelling from inside the house. I was ripped off my horse and screamed at for doing something so careless and dangerous and warned never to do anything like that again. I was at a loss. Everyone was disappointed in me. My horse was finally doing things I wanted, and it looked like I might be able to go somewhere with it, but I was so confused by the internal conflict I was experiencing at all levels from my external feedback.

It was clear I wasn't enjoying my arena work anymore, and all the people helping me were at a loss. They had decided I was lazy and wasn't going to make it in the horse world if I kept this up. They had started poking fun at me because I found comfort in climbing up on Katy's bare back while she was in her pen without any tack on and falling asleep on her. They no longer believed I was serious about learning to ride and train horses, and they were tired of wasting their time on me. I decided to prove them wrong.

Up until that point, I had to walk Katy on foot through the arena gate because she would refuse to enter the gate for me while I was on her back. At the time, it never occurred to me that it might mean she absolutely abhorred what awaited her on the other side of that gate. I was told that if I didn't get the upper hand with her and win that battle, I would never be able to do much with horses. I was told to kick and kick and continue to kick until I won. If I just kept kicking, eventually one of us would give in, and it had to be her; otherwise, Katy would always take advantage of me, and I wouldn't be able to get her or any other horse to do anything. So that afternoon, as we headed to the gate and she began to stall, I started kicking. I kicked and kicked and kicked. I kicked until my legs went to jelly. I kicked until the sun went down, literally. And after what seemed like forever, with a very pissed-off red horse underneath me, Katy gave in and moved through the gate. Both of us drenched in sweat, we passed under the glow of the arena lights into the sand ahead. I rewarded her with tons of praise and petting, and a huge smile inched across my face. I could barely walk, but as I stumbled into the house to tell everyone what had just happened—that I had just won the GREAT BATTLE—I was beaming with pride because I knew they'd be proud of me. I was right.

The power that coursed through my body as we reached the point where Katy gave in and I got what I wanted was nothing less than intoxicating. I felt so strong. I had taken complete control of something for the first time in my life. Control of my life was something I craved more than anything else. It meant I didn't have to be so sad and afraid, which is why I was so angry. I learned a valuable lesson that night, one that would provide great returns for me over the next several years. I already knew how to make money selling horses, and that night I learned that

if I could kick or hit longer or harder than the horse was willing to fight, or just be more persistent in general, then I would
eventually win and that horse would never challenge me again. I
learned to break horses that night, starting with the one horse I
had fallen in love with. So began a new love affair—my love for
power and control.

FOUR

-El Rancho Learna Lotta-

"Violence is the last refuge of the incompetent."
~ Isaac Asimov

{*There was always a flutter in my belly when one of the ranch geldings and I would approach the edge of the cliff where the trail led down to the river. A slight anxiety would arise as I would anticipate either the fight that would ensue or the achievement of submission from the horse as he finally accepted I was in charge. I never lost a battle with one of them. Katy had prepared me well for what it took, but when the battle didn't actually happen, THAT was a sure sign that I had won. When we would reach the drop and the horse would just sigh and continue without hesitation over the edge and down the first steep slope of the switchback, that's when I knew I was doing my job well and that the horses would safely and willingly carry whomever I put on their backs down to the river. That's what I was being paid for, after all.*

One afternoon, things didn't go as planned. You balked. You reared. You flipped around, and you began to back up—right over the edge. I took the reins to your hide and kicked as hard as I could to push you forward again, but it was too late. Up, up, and over backwards you came, down on top of me, and we rolled down the stretch together, end over end. You recovered much faster than I, and you headed back up the hill and around the corner, surely leaving me in the dirt to walk with my head hung low in shame over a mile back to the barn, where I was sure you would be waiting.

Once I could breathe again, I stood up and began to trudge up the hill. Defeated, in pain, and so angry at myself and at you for leaving me, I was immobilized as I lifted my eyes and saw you standing at the top. You had come back. You had walked away, headed back home, and then changed your plan and returned to me. I had hurt you. I had said hateful things. I tried to force you to do something you clearly didn't want to do. Yet, you returned—and you carried me. Why would you do that, gentle Paint? Why would you do that?}

+++++++++++++

As I entered my senior year of high school, a lot of changes were underway. I now boarded Katy at a family friend's place because my father and the woman with the horse trainer parents had broken up. I finally had a horse I could ride who basically did anything I asked of her, but horses had taken a backburner to the drama that was my relationship with my boyfriend and the balancing of that with my disapproving father. I knew I wanted to work with horses after high school, but I had less support in that than ever before after it was decided that I was ultimately too lazy to do what it took. Not to mention, now that my father no longer had any ties to the horse world, to him my obsession was back to being a waste of time and energy.

I took a job in a local pawn shop as I began college. The job itself was really fun and interesting, but I was working for an older, sometimes more daunting, version of my father. In fact, my boss and my father were good friends. I learned a great deal at that job, usually the hard way. My sales and negotiation skills were honed, and my confidence grew in dealing with the public as I was regularly forced into situations with customers that didn't give me the chance to run away. I really did learn valuable skills during that employment, but more than once those lessons were plastered down my cheeks in the form of tears and evenings of despair. The people mostly in charge of my life were tired of my talking about horses, and I was told repeatedly how I could never make a living working with horses. They wanted me to learn how to run and manage the pawn shop instead—but if the lack of peace and happiness in my boss was what I had to look forward to going down that road, then no thanks. I wanted out. I was desperate to find a job with horses, but my experience was mostly limited to my small achievements with Fancy and Katy.

One awesome benefit to working at the pawn shop was the variety of local people I got to meet. Many people saw something in me worth giving their attention to, and I was friendly with all of my co-workers as well. At the risk of pissing off the boss, one of the part-time guys, who was good friends with the management, slipped me a piece of paper with a name and number on it one day. He told me to give the guy on the paper a call. There was a big ranch just outside of town looking for someone to ride the guest horses. Jackpot!

I made the call, and a few days later, I showed up determined to take advantage of a perfect opportunity. The place was a private 500-acre guest ranch that a Dallas businessman owned and used to entertain family and friends. They had a string of four ranch geldings that had become difficult for inexperienced guests to ride as there was no one to keep them tuned up. That's what my job would be—to keep the horses ridden and ready for guests and to lead trail rides whenever needed. For my interview, I was asked to catch, saddle, and ride one of the horses. Lupe was a 16-hand-high monster of a quarter horse. I had never been so close to a horse like this. He looked and smelled like money— way more money than I would ever spend on a horse. It took everything I had to lug over one of the ranch's heavy roping saddles and lift it onto his back—a back that stood eye-level high to me—but I was able to get it done.

The owner and I rode around a bit talking, and I got the job. I finally had my first real job with horses as a wrangler and trail guide. I would show up four to six days a week after my college classes and ride these amazing animals around an equally amazing piece of property. I could not believe someone was paying me to do this. Not only was I getting paid to ride awesome horses, but this ranch was just incredible. A $1.5 million log cabin was the main house, and it sat on the edge of a cliff overlooking the Brazos River. There was a steep switchback trail down to the water, and I would take the horses down that trail and lose myself for hours in what I was sure was Heaven on Earth. I would daydream about what it must have been like to have grown up with so much nature to play in, and I was grateful for every second of the time I spent there.

This time in my life is when my real education and experience with horses began. I had complete autonomy with the horses and their care, and for the next year they taught me so much. Their compliance under saddle improved dramatically, and my boss was very happy with my horsemanship skills and reliability. He would regularly call me on weekends to have horses saddled and ready for his guests, and I'd spend hours leading them around the ranch and having lively conversations, frequently getting praise for my skill on horseback but also for my personality, passion, and articulation of the things I cared about and found interesting. These times were my main source of support during that period, and my confidence began to grow and grow as my talent with the horses got more and more developed.

I can only think of one reason that set me apart from others where my skill with horses was concerned. I was fearless. I didn't care about getting hurt. You could almost say I welcomed it. I had experienced so much pain in life already that the threat of hitting the ground wasn't all that scary to me. I did learn how to hit the ground, though. Before the job at the ranch, I had never really been bucked off before. It took a few times to figure out how to avoid it, but I got pretty good at keeping my ass in that saddle. Boss taught me the most, and to this day he's one of my all-time favorite horses. He was the dominant horse in the herd and had been a stallion for the first nine years of his life. I adored him. He was big, strong, and handsome, and boy was he a jerk. We understood each other pretty well. No one else liked him because of his aggression, but even without knowing why or realizing it at the time, I recognized myself in him. He was so strong, and he didn't like it when anyone told him how to be or what to do. He loved freedom as much as I did. I grew to love him quickly, and I trusted him completely no matter how many times I'd been hurt by him.

One time, I was walking behind him near the barn as I was saddling up the horses to take two adorable children out for a ride. He mistook me for one of the other horses and kicked out hard, and I was completely unprepared for it. He nailed me right in the leg. Of course, at that time, my answer for such situations was to pay him back with the same kind of energy, so I kicked him back, at least three times, as hard as I could. The children I was about to take riding stared in horror. I explained how it was important for me to do that because that's what he understood, and by doing the same thing he would have done, it made me look like the leader in his eyes. This was horse philosophy as I knew it at the time, as many people understood it actually, and even as the words came out of my mouth, something in my body screamed. I didn't know what that meant, or even how to recognize it, so I just stuffed it down and resumed my position of authority on the subject. The kids just nodded quietly, and we went on our ride. Later that weekend, they made cards thanking me for their adventure and apologizing that Boss had been so mean to me. I'd give a lot to go back and change the lesson I extended to those boys that day.

Another time, Boss and I were far away from the barn and I'd had a particularly bad day at school, so I was listening to music with my headphones on as we plodded around the ranch, exploring and working on reining. Suddenly, he just broke into a wild, bucking frenzy. I didn't have a chance. I had 1300 pounds of raw power and muscle going crazy underneath me. I still have no idea what set him off, but I landed hard on some rocks, and he took off like a rocket. Oh, was I mad. I thought we were friends! I was so incredibly pissed, not to mention that it hurt like hell, and as I stomped off to find him, I was seething the entire way. I don't know how long it took me to find him on the edge of the woods, but I walked right up to him and punched him hard, right in the face. He didn't run away. It was an interesting exchange, but I felt we were even; I hopped back on, and we finished our ride without further incident.

Getting bucked off wasn't something I wanted to keep happening, especially from the back of the giant and powerful ranch horses. I had to figure it out, but so far I hadn't been able to figure out just what it was that needed to happen in order for me to stay on. They were so big and so fast, and if I lost my balance at all, I typically checked out and just allowed myself to be thrown since I was fairly good at tucking and rolling once I hit the ground. Sometimes I even landed on my feet. The issue was that I didn't want them to learn that bucking was a solution to getting out of work, and I definitely didn't want to spend my afternoons walking around looking for my horse! Boss gave me the opportunity I needed. I felt it coming, and I was committed to staying in the fight instead of giving up and falling off to the safety of a roll. I got angry. I let my anger consume me, and it gave me strength. I held on, I pulled his head sideways, and I rode that big monster until he stopped. We then went on our merry way without any more issues. It wasn't the last time a horse bucked me, but it was the first time that I realized I had everything it took to stay on. Just like when Katy didn't want to enter the arena, I remembered that if I was more persistent, and tougher, the horse would always give in, as long as I could stay in the fight. Smaller horses, and most of them were, after that were not very scary—no matter what they tried to unleash on me.

Probably the most powerful lesson of that year came in the form of a huge scar on my left calf. The lesson had nothing to do with horses, actually, though Boss was the one to deliver it. This might sound a little crazy, but I had been reading a Dean Koontz novel at the time where the killer in the story had increased his pain tolerance exponentially by practicing on himself. That way, when his victims would fight back, he would be able to continue without the pain getting in the way. I found this whole concept very interesting—not the morbid and psychotic aspect of why he was doing it, but the idea that suffering was optional and that pain, when looked at with non-judgment and acceptance, could be tolerated at very high levels. As someone who suffered greatly in life thus far, the idea that suffering might be optional, even if only on the physical level, was something I wanted to know about. One day, Boss was tired of me being on his back, so he decided to brush up against a barbed wire fence in an attempt to get rid of me. Having just read the book, and being in a pretty depressed state with my life outside of horses in general, I made a conscious choice to let the barbed wire make full contact with my leg. I would just watch it. I wouldn't judge it as a bad experience; I would simply witness the metal barb tearing through my flesh. And it did. It was a warm, autumn day with a light breeze. I was wearing shorts, and we moved through tall grass before reaching the fence line. I dropped my hands and gave Boss full control as he moved up against the taut barbed wire. I stared blankly at my leg as the metal barb connected and penetrated my skin, tearing my leg open in a straight line as we walked forward together. Blood ran down my leg as Boss moved away from the fence line. I felt a little crazy, and I knew no one would understand what I had just done, but the interesting thing was—it didn't hurt. I knew in a lot of ways it was probably a really stupid experiment, but at the same time, I had just discovered something truly important. Pain only leads to suffering when we judge it as a negative experience or resist it. This stayed with me. When I rode back up to the barn, the guys that were working rushed out to aid me. I didn't tell them exactly what happened or why, so I just acted tough and got a pat on the back for being a bad ass—and a smack in the head for being a dumb ass.

Day in, day out, I rode the ranch horses and learned how to control them, how to work with them, and how to get them to willingly do what I asked through repetition and reward. We rescued baby lambs together, we swam in the river together, we encountered wild animals and harsh terrain, and we met every challenge imaginable together. The experience I gained through that first year on those amazing geldings was invaluable, and it turned me into one hell of a rider. It brought joy to my life and a chance to be truly grateful for something—and great AT something. I loved those horses dearly, and I loved the work. However,

I wasn't making much money, and I knew I couldn't make a life riding horses around for six bucks an hour. I decided to let my boss in on a little secret of mine. I knew how to pick, buy, and sell horses, and I knew how to do it profitably.

FIVE

-Horsemanship Isn't Natural-

*"The only thing that climbs on a horse's back in nature is
the cougar about to eat him."*
~ Dale Moulton

{I hadn't seen you in the corrals outside, but when you walked into the ring, I knew you were going home with me. It was a packed house as usual, and my heart started racing as I wondered who I would be competing against for the top bid to take you away. The auctioneer gave us your stats. Six years old, not broke to ride, Percheron crossed with 78% foundation Quarter Horse. The most beautiful red roan I'd ever seen. You were 16.2 hands high, around 1500 lbs., and a stallion. I smiled. Right away I knew that you were everyone in that room's worst nightmare, but you were my dream come true.

There were snickers and muffled laughter when some of the men noticed the young girl in the back bidding on you. That reaction always made me smile. They saw an accident waiting to happen. I knew it to be my competitive edge. You see, most of the horse traders in the room were old men who had to hire young cowboys to train the horses they would be selling. Not me. I trained everything myself, and there wasn't a horse I couldn't handle. Not even you. There weren't very many people in the bidding seats prepared to take on a stallion, much less one of your size and age, so it wasn't much of a surprise that I purchased you with a winning bid of only $550.

I raced out to the corrals to meet you before the auctioneer's "SOLD" finished ringing in my ears. They had run you into a pen next to a mare that was in heat, and you were getting a little excited. I walked right up to you, and you turned to face me. I was cocky and proud, and I had just purchased my first stallion to prove what I was made of. I put the halter on you, and you resisted so that you could go back to the mare. I demanded you come with me instead. You walked right up to me, looked me in the eye, and in a flash threw out one of your front hooves and struck me to the ground clear to the other side of the pen. Shit. What had I gotten myself into?

I drove home without you, freaking out that I had made a huge mistake and been a little overconfident in my capabilities as a trainer. I had never worked with a stallion, much less started an aged one under saddle. You had already hurt me, and I barely knew you. I sat on my living room floor, crying and feeling sorry for myself. Then I realized that I had to go back and get you or I would be a laughingstock. I waited until everyone had left the sale barn, late at night, to return to you. I brought my training stick. When I entered your pen again, you immediately charged me, and my training stick met you with perfect timing across the cheek, and hard. You walked right onto my trailer and never hurt me again.

I fell in love with your power, your essence, your everything. We became friends, and I would climb up on the pipe fence around the barn where I could sit and brush your forelock and stare into your big, amazing eyes—because I couldn't reach you from the ground. There was something magical about stallions, and you were proof. Maybe the magic was that I could control you. I only amounted to 10% of your total weight, and yet I could command you, and you listened. I used you to show off. I used you to impress others. I used you. Somewhere underneath that, however, I loved you more deeply than any other horse I had ever met. You were only business, though, and when I was done training you—when I was done taking your power away from you— you were sold, just like the others. You went to Virginia, and still to this day, after all the horses that have come and gone, you're the one I regret losing the most.}

+++++++++++++

Most kids in college spend their weekends partying, socializing, or at least studying. Not me. My Friday and Saturday nights were usually spent at public horse auctions. During my first year of riding horses for the ranch, I had bought and sold a couple of horses for myself and made a huge profit again, just like with Fancy. When I explained this to my boss, he saw an opportunity both to help me do what I enjoyed and to also have a tax-deductible expense for the ranch business. So we worked out a deal where I would earn a commission for horses that I brokered for the ranch, and I would pay a commission for horses I bought and sold for myself, keeping them on ranch property.

It was a sweet deal indeed, and he'd send me to the week-end sales with a blank check to do with as I pleased. I rarely ever came home empty-handed. Sometimes I would have to make two trips with my trailer to get the new horses home, and one time I convinced an adorable pony to ride in my tack room so I wouldn't have to make the extra trip. That was particularly impressive to guys working the corrals that night.

Some horses I kept for a couple of months; others sold within a week. I once bought a pretty, little grey mare, unseen, off the internet. I called the seller up, offered him $700 cash based on the description, met him on the side of the highway, and took less than ten minutes to unload her out of his trailer and reload her into mine. Two weeks later, and after many rides to see what she knew, I sold her for $1,800 to a very happy buyer. I knew exactly the right questions to ask a seller to know what I was getting and if any lies were being told about the horse's health. I didn't care about any behavior or training issues, as everyone has their own opinions where that is concerned, and I would work that out between myself and the horse. My sales goal was to be able to price the horses at 100% over my cost and sell them before 50% of the profit was eaten up with expenses. It worked more often than not. I was flipping horses like crazy and had become pretty well-known as a source for decently trained, and often beautiful, trail horses. It was the perfect scenario—I had the money to buy them, the hours to ride them, and the perfect place to do all the training and marketing. The ranch offered both the horses and me infinite and varied experiences and learn-ing opportunities, so that with each ride they became more mar-ketable and I became more skilled as a trainer.

Within the next two years, I had bought, trained, and sold over 100 different horses. They came from all different back-grounds, breeds, training, and circumstances. There was no bet-ter education for me, and learning directly from my experiences with all of those individual horses gave me a solid foundation from which to question everything anyone else ever tried to tell me about horses or how to train them. It was just me and the horses most of the time, with very little outside influence, until I decided to seek it on my own.

To appease my father, I went to school for business management rather than horses. It was a smart move, and it made me great at selling horses. I was honest and reliable, and I knew the importance of good customer service. I also cared about the horses, so I wouldn't hesitate to tell someone no if I didn't think they'd be a good fit with whatever horse they were interested in. Each horse had an elaborate evaluation form that covered general information about them as well as their health records, and it went on to cover every area of training and experience so that potential buyers could know exactly what to expect from each horse and what their strengths and weaknesses were both on the ground and under saddle. I was also into web design at the time, and way back before a lot of people were using much video or fancy HTML on their sites, I was getting over 1000 hits a month, mostly from women who enjoyed looking at the photos and videos of the horses I had for sale. Most of my sales were made through internet classifieds and my website. If I wasn't at school, I was riding, selling, or hauling horses.

My life at home had become miserable and filled with chaos and despair. I had moved out of my father's house, which in many ways was probably a huge mistake, and moved right in with my boyfriend. This hurt my relationship with my father more than I could have understood at the time. My boyfriend and I fought constantly, but we were so attached that the comfort between us kept me completely paralyzed to considering anything else. My self-esteem plummeted, I gained a lot of weight, and if it weren't for the horses and my dogs, I might have killed myself. The animals were the only relationships I had ever had that offered me a constant source of loving kindness from another being. I met the deepest, darkest edges of despair in those days. The person I loved most was horrible to me, and I to him. How can two people care so much for one another and yet treat one another so very bad? It still breaks my heart that people mistake this kind of relationship for love. Before the age of 20, I knew what it was to hit absolute rock bottom and not want to live anymore. I relied on the horses and my school studies to keep my head afloat.

I did a good amount of traveling during those days. I'd drive just about anywhere if it meant I could get a great deal on a horse that I could make some money on. I mostly drove all over Texas and Oklahoma, picking horses up wherever I found them cheapest. It was my first real taste of independence, and it made me feel confident and strong to be able to work these business deals and hook up my truck and trailer by myself, handling the horses the way I did. The horses, as always, were my escape from facing my past, dealing with the horrible problems at home, or myself in general. Only now, my escape came with money and power as well. My success was giving me a big head, and since the horses were mostly a commodity in my world, I missed out on a lot of what they were trying to tell me.

A big sale came through one February for one of the most beautiful horses I ever owned. Apache was a very flashy, and sometimes headstrong, palomino Paint gelding. The girl that purchased him lived in Wisconsin, and when she asked me if I knew any good commercial haulers, on a whim I offered to do it myself. I was ready for an adventure, I suppose. Not wanting to make such a big trip to return empty-handed, I looked for horses online anywhere between Wisconsin and Texas and found one I wanted to purchase on the way back—a gorgeous, smoky buckskin named Frosty King, who was half mustang, in Iowa. I had never driven that far before, much less to Northern states in the winter, but the plan was to leave Friday, haul my gelding to Wisconsin after a quick sleepover in Missouri, and immediately hit the road to Iowa with plans to get back to Texas before Monday. After sleepless nights, more snow than I had ever seen, and below-zero temperatures, I made it to Iowa on time just for my new horse to refuse to get in the trailer.

Frosty King's owner, Nikki, and I hit it off instantly. We decided to take a break from trying to get him in the trailer in order to keep our fingers and everything else from freezing off. We ordered a pizza and went inside to get to know one another. Nikki was the first other female I had ever connected with on so many levels, and so quickly. We really had a lot in common, and I ended up spending the day with her. She was very excited to introduce me via DVD to this new trainer and his method that she was studying. Natural Horsemanship was a relatively new term at the time, with only two well-known players in the industry. I knew of one of them and had studied him quite a bit; I believe he coined the term Natural Horsemanship, actually. I was really turned off by his presentation, so I never took the time to apply his methods, though I did study them in great detail. This new guy on the scene, which my new friend was introducing to me, was exciting. He was practical and told it like it was. I admired his direct and honest approach. He was also quite cute with an even cuter accent, so with the money I had left over from selling my gelding and purchasing Frosty King, I invested in his entire DVD training program after one afternoon of watching him on Nikki's couch.

My new horse decided he was ready to load by the time we were finished visiting, so I set off back home for Texas and made it by the wee hours of Monday morning. It was time to take things to another level with this interesting new concept of Natural Horsemanship.

SIX

-Equine "Science"-

"The important thing is to never stop questioning."
~ Albert Einstein

{It was dark in the arena where the round pen had been placed behind the bleachers. The lights hanging from the ceiling seemed to swing like a dimly lit chandelier in the dining room of a haunted house, though I'm sure they weren't moving at all. I nervously led you into the pen, followed by three of my fellow classmates, one with a video camera in hand.

You were the first horse whose only training had been from me. You were the first colt I ever started. I knew that whatever was about to happen would be directly related to what I had put into our time together. I was scared, and I had an audience. For as much as I liked to run my mouth to make up for everything I lacked in genuine confidence, we were all about to find out how well I lived up to my own words where horses were concerned.

The other girls climbed onto the panels to watch us as I moved you gently into the center of the pen. I was anxious, and I had no intention of preparing you any further right then. We had spent months doing that already. My heart was racing; I could hear it and feel it in my ears. Ba boom ba boom ba boom! I turned your nose into the saddle the way I had learned would keep me safe should you try to buck. I held my breath and whispered words I don't recall as I placed my left foot in the stirrup and lifted off the ground. My right leg swung over your back as my butt landed gently in the saddle. I took one, long, deep breath as I sat deep and relaxed my legs with my shoulders rounded and ready for anything, and I asked you to walk forward.

You got a little nervous at the first request but quickly got it together and moved forward. We walked together, both directions, turning each way around the pen, and you stopped like a perfect gentleman. We did it. You were perfect. I was the first person in class to ride my colt, and unlike the others, you didn't even buck. Not once. They all thought it was because you were too gentle, but I knew what we had done to earn this, and I remember when you challenged me and tried to push me around in the beginning, but not anymore. I had tried to understand you, and I had been able to show you that if you did what I asked, it would be so easy, and you wouldn't be hurt.

I never got over the rush of that first ride—the few moments between my feet leaving the ground and my butt hitting the saddle, anticipating what would happen next. Either you would buck, which clearly meant I had failed at preparing you for being ridden, or you would bravely accept my request, indicating that I had done a good job and earned your trust. At least that's the way I understood it at the time. You were the first, but that rush was there with every single horse after you, and it became my new addiction. When I started them myself, I knew everything that happened was a reflection of the work I had done, and I could use that feedback to build my confidence. My inner world was more and more becoming dependent on the outside of a horse.}

+++++++++++++

It wasn't until my senior year of college that I was able to add equine science to my curriculum. Up until that point, I had promised to dedicate my studies to business, and I had fulfilled that commitment, as well as the prerequisites for the Equine Training Program. I had never started a young horse under saddle, and most of my horse training at that point was tuning up and "fixing" horses that had already been broke to ride, or at least started at some point. I was beyond excited to add this to my experience because I felt that the key to making real money was to be able to pick them young, when they were really inexpensive, and train them to my own personal standard without any outside influence. Then I would know absolutely everything about them and everything that had gone into them, which would make them easier to sell at the price I wanted. I had no idea how exciting it would also be, and that was just icing on the cake. That first ride on a colt was the stuff adrenaline junkies are born from.

Natural Horsemanship had only barely begun to reach the curriculum of my school's horse training program. I did not agree with much of what I was being asked to do, having done my own study at home through my DVD program with the cute young Aussie I was introduced to in Iowa. The school's tactics were a little harsher than what I was learning on my own, but that wasn't the part that bothered me so much. Quite simply, the methods I was learning worked better because they got consistent results faster, and though it was nice to be gentler with the horses, it was the efficiency of the methodology that was most important to me. I was in the business of selling the horses as quickly as possible for the most amount of money, after all, so the faster the training worked, the better. Also, I wasn't trying to be a bronco rider any more, and I liked how the methods I was using pretty much guaranteed I wouldn't get bucked off if I applied them correctly.

I was matched with a headstrong little grey colt named Dusty, and my life was changed. Most of the horses I had worked with up until then were gone within a few weeks, so I wasn't expecting what would happen when I had a horse to spend so much consistent time with and be held accountable for his progress over a specific time frame. Katy was the only horse I had ever held onto very long, and even that was quite inconsistent, filled with so much ignorance, and resulted in my selling her my second year at the ranch. Dusty would be the first horse that I was absolutely committed to with my new experience level and knowledge for at least a year. He was also a fine colt in breeding and conformation and gorgeous with his black mane and tail, so of course I purchased him for his $2,500 asking price, which his breeder and our assistant professor allowed me to pay out over the length of the curriculum. To this day, I have never paid that much for another horse.

I followed the curriculum diligently, though I often replaced the training methods dictated in class for those I was using and learning at home and in my business. This got me noticed quite often, and not always in a positive light. The professor in charge of the program wasn't the least bit impressed with me. I was chubby, inexperienced, and arrogant, and since I had never competed and didn't come from a background with horses, my direct opposition to some of what I was being taught brought ridicule upon me rather than interest. One day on my way to class I saw my professor in a stall with one of the colts, reprimanding him for something. He was standing in the doorway of the stall, and every time the colt would do something other than what was wanted, he would whip him. The poor horse was in a box stall with no way of avoiding the punishment other than to do what was expected of him. I didn't know much, but I knew that seemed ridiculously unfair and brutal, and I didn't want this man's help with training my colt—especially since he was indeed MY colt.

I always exceeded the week's training goals using the more natural methods I was learning. Basically, the point behind Natural Horsemanship was to bring in the science and natural behavior of horses to be applied in their training rather than relying solely on force, which traditionally had been the accepted way until this so-called revolution in horsemanship began. It was modeled after the herd dynamics of wild horses, assuming a dominant horse would remain in charge if he could control the movement of another horse's feet. I won't go into too much detail as there are plenty of materials on the subject already, but faulty science or not, it absolutely worked to get results. Unfortunately, while this understanding of working with horses was gaining in popularity and being used, it was teamed with words and concepts like trust, relationship, respect, cooperation, and, worst of all, love. I bought into it wholeheartedly along with millions of others.

As my training techniques softened and became very consistent, Dusty got softer and more willing in all of my requests. We were doing very well together, and I was really happy with his progress. He was becoming exactly the horse I wanted him to be. My professor and some of the other students would sneer at us and tell me how lucky I was to get such a "dead head" since they were having a lot of problems with their colts, some even getting bucked off. I was the first student to ride my colt that semester, and it went perfectly. How quickly they forgot that when we were all picking our colts in the beginning, Dusty was considered one of the more difficult ones to work with because he was so bossy. Instead of being congratulated, I was often criticized for the both of us being too lazy. I was warned that he would probably blow up on me at any point because I obviously wasn't demanding enough of him if he was being so willing and accepting of everything. It really messed with my head, but I had no intention of changing what I was doing, because it was working for us; and since he was mine, that was most important.

Because I was purchasing him, I was allowed to take Dusty home over the winter break. For his third ride, I used him to lead a group trail ride at my ranch job, in only a halter and a bareback pad. He was fabulous. No one believed me that it was only his third ride. I believed I was a pretty good trainer with the horses before, but with this I had found something I might truly be great at. Starting colts, even if this was only the first time, seemed to be my forte, and I loved it. What wasn't to love? I was a control freak, and starting them myself gave me control over a lot more of the process.

When we returned for the spring semester and the advanced portion of the training class, I was so happy with my horse. He did absolutely anything I asked, and I trusted him completely to keep me safe. While other students were getting bucked off or frustrated with their colts, I'd be standing on Dusty's back in the middle of the arena, being an asshole and showing off. He was so good that I was allowed to use him in my evening equitation class alongside much older and more seasoned horses. He was the only colt allowed in that class; it was designed to teach us how to ride better, which meant they wanted horses that were well trained. That class turned out to be very helpful in my business, as well, since I'd often bring horses I had in training and use them for my practical exams.

Internally, I was thrilled with my success with Dusty and couldn't have been much happier with myself. Not everyone felt that way, though. The professor in charge of the program and the department head weren't impressed with us at all. Dusty was to be an all-around trail horse, so I didn't push him to cut and sort cows, and I didn't want to wear spurs to make him move to the side fast, like we were encouraged to do. As long as he did what I asked, I was happy. That earned us a big fat B as an overall grade that semester, along with a personal report that we were lazy and that Dusty was unpredictable because he'd never been pushed, which made him dangerous and an accident waiting to happen. I was also informed that because of my example, no student would ever be allowed to use their personal horses in the training program again.

A month later, we held the annual spring sale where all of the training colts were auctioned off. I used my business and reputation as a trader to advertise and spread the word, helping to make it the most successful sale in the school's history. I knew I had a gift for working with horses, and my experiences gave me the proof outside of anyone else's opinions. The colt my professor trained alongside us brought $4,000 at the spring sale. When I sold Dusty the following year, he brought an easy $6,500. I kept that final review of Dusty and me, and it fueled a wild fire inside me. The fire that grew was my new firm understanding that just because someone may be an expert in the ways that once were does not mean they are an authority on the way that things can be.

SEVEN

-Lesson from the Buddha-

"Believe nothing, no matter where you read it, or who said it, no matter if I have said it, unless it agrees with your own reason and your own common sense."
~ Buddha

{I don't even remember where you came from, but there was always something unique and special about you. Not knowing much about Buddhism other than what I learned in cultural studies back in high school, I have no idea why I was inclined to name you Buddha. It just popped in my head after meeting you. Such a handsome little palomino. Our time together was brief, but your impact and sacrifice left an impression that shall never fade.

That afternoon changed the course of my future, thanks to you. I sat atop another horse, about 100 feet away, watching as my training partner began your lesson for the day. You had been giving us some trouble, so we had dedicated the afternoon to convincing you that your life would be easier if we could all come to a better understanding. You had the looks that would sell, but your attitude needed to be greatly improved first.

I relaxed in my saddle to watch what could be done to improve things with you. Within a short period, you made a decision that caused my body to fill with tension. You did the one thing that was never acceptable from a horse and from my experience always resulted in an ugly scene. Instead of fighting back—you decided to shut down. You lay down with a trainer on your back and refused to move. I didn't have to have my eyes open to see the anger move in. I could feel it. I watched as my partner turned into a monster I knew very well. It was that point when—once all known efforts have been exhausted—frustration sets in, and violence takes over. The reins became weapons, and I watched in horror as, lash after lash, whelps developed upon your hide. You didn't move a muscle.

I sat in total silence, watching the mirror of what I had become. It didn't matter that it wasn't me inflicting your pain that day, because I had done it to others and knew the scene well. Only, something had changed in me, and this time, as I stared, I saw myself reflected back, and I did not want to be that person any longer. In our world, what was happening was considered an entirely appropriate response to your decision to lie down and quit trying. We had been taught to react this way by respected horsemen of our time, to punish you for such disrespect.

However, love had recently entered my life in a profound way, and I simply saw things differently now.

I took over your training after that day, apologizing silently to you at every opportunity, even when I startled you one day and ended up being thrown off your back. You changed everything as I watched you be beaten, in the same way I had been taught to punish you, for what was at that time considered to be the absolute worst thing a horse could do—to outright say no and refuse to be controlled, without fighting back. Thank you for saying "no more." I'm not sure how many more "no's" I might have ignored if it weren't for your lesson that day.}

+++++++++++++

I graduated college with honors, but I didn't walk across the stage, and I didn't invite anyone to my graduation. School and the horses were a life completely separate from the mess I lived in at home, and they were sacred to me. I claimed full responsibility for all of my academic and business success, and I didn't want to share it with anyone I was still so profoundly angry with. My boyfriend and I had become engaged, and I had surrendered to the idea that my personal life was simply destined to be doomed, but I had the horses at least. With no example of loving human relationships to learn from firsthand, how could it be otherwise? Somehow, by surrendering to my current situation, I gained the courage to move forward into the unknown. As my confidence grew from the horses, I wanted more for myself, and I decided to reach out and make a new friend—a friendship that maybe for the first time wouldn't just happen naturally in a school setting but would require effort. I reached out, taking everything I had learned from my many years of trying to make a doomed relationship work with my boyfriend and combining it with everything I had learned about cooperating with horses, and I made my first adult best friend. At 21, I did indeed die as my palm had indicated all those years back in grade school, but it was just the first of many deaths to come—a death that would lead to rising into a new life and way of being.

True love had finally entered my life in the form of my new friend. I had yet to experience love on this level before, and it affected me in many unexpected ways. I met Brandy outside of the arena for that first horse training class. I was instantly drawn to her, and I felt safe around her. We mucked stalls together, we studied together, and we laughed together—a lot. Suddenly, I had someone in my life who cared for me without expectation or demands—someone who was there whenever I needed her and always met me at least half way. I felt truly safe with someone for the first time, and it softened me so much that the wall I had built up developed a painful crack for all the world to see. My health improved, and I developed confidence outside of horses for the first time as an adult. Life was beginning to be fun and exciting, and I felt hopeful. I felt beautiful and emotionally fulfilled in a way I had not yet experienced.

Right out of college, I partnered up with a talented young trainer named Kris. We continued my business together—buying, training, and selling horses. At this point, we had really adopted and become skilled at the concepts of Natural Horsemanship and were a talented duo. I would start the horses under saddle, and she would finish them in more refined areas, targeting whatever talents they possessed. Unfortunately, we joined forces during a very tumultuous period of change in my life, in more ways than one.

As Brandy and I grew closer over the next year and developed the first real relationship based on love and trust for both of us, we fell IN love. I never knew I could fall in love with another woman. I remember being attracted to both boys and girls equally when I was young, but at 13 I began dating the same boy I was with when I met Brandy, so the idea of being with another woman had never really been entertained before then. I went through a period in high school where I wondered if I was gay, but it was all very confusing because I knew I was attracted to boys too. I was embarrassed and scared to explore it.

Bisexuality was not something I was prepared to understand in my little Texas town with my early Southern Baptist conditioning, so I just shut it down and tried to make my more socially acceptable relationship with my boyfriend work. As is true of so many things, it was more acceptable to most for me to be unhappy with a man than living joyfully with another woman. After nine years of mostly turmoil, I decided to leave my boyfriend and start a new life with Brandy, the woman I had fallen for.

This affected my life in every way imaginable, including my horse training. I had softened a great deal and become much more sensitive through my enhanced sensitivity toward my new girlfriend. I was beginning to see things in my training methods that no longer felt good. Even though the training methods we used on the horses were considered very gentle for the time, even weak to many traditional horsemen, they no longer seemed all that gentle to me. When I watched one afternoon as Kris took the reins and beat a little palomino gelding for shutting down on her, I saw with horror what I had become. I couldn't do it any more, not like this. I needed time to explore the changes within me, and since my life as I knew it was unraveling anyway, it was a good opportunity to close up shop with everyone I was currently working with in the horse world.

My business partnership with Kris and with the ranch dissolved. I burned a lot of bridges over the next few months as I left it all behind to seek happiness with another woman in a new town. All of my business partners claimed to be devout Christians, and none of the decisions I was making were going over very well with any of them. I was also running away and ending agreements much more prematurely than I had intended. My spirits were lifted very unexpectedly one night at the sale barn as I was getting ready to bid on a new horse to train and sell. My phone rang, and I was surprised to look down and see "Dad" on the screen. It wasn't common for him to call me, so I rushed into the lobby where I could hear him. I had not yet told him about the true nature of my relationship with my "best friend" as I was terrified of his response—not just to my being with another woman, but for jumping immediately into another relationship directly out of the one that had already caused so much tension between him and me. I had, however, told his girlfriend, and apparently she had ratted me out. His response, and his reason for calling me that night, stunned me. He had called to tell me he knew the truth and that he was proud of me and happy for me. I couldn't believe the words I had just heard. This moment marked the beginning of a very long journey of healing between my father and me, and it filled my heart more than he probably knew at the time. It did help that everyone who met Brandy fell absolutely in love with her as well.

So, once the bridges of my old life were ablaze, I set out to begin a new life as an openly gay woman in the horse industry. I'm not much for labels these days, but back then I was flying my rainbow flag high and proud. I left my hometown to live somewhere else for the very first time, and I finally felt like a truly independent young woman. I was on top of the world for a while. I took my horse training business solo again with an entirely different perspective on how to work with the animals. Love had opened me up, and relationships became my primary concern in every endeavor with the horses and in my life. I also put more emphasis on starting colts rather than correcting problems with already seasoned horses. This shift brought many joyful moments, making that year one filled with amazing memories, despite how stressful it was with the massive amount of change I was experiencing. I will always look back on that time of my life with a full heart and a huge smile.

The buying, training, and selling was going relatively well— except for one thing. More than ever before, I was getting really inconsistent results once the horse moved on to another owner. Sometimes the person would have no problems and be very happy with the horse they had purchased. Other times, I would receive a phone call about a month later with someone on the other end complaining a horse I had sold them had just tried to kill them. Then they would go on to describe a situation that I could simply not fathom, given what I knew about that particular horse. This continued for months, and I could not understand what was happening.

Unknowingly, I had abandoned focused technique and consistency in my training for in-the-moment responses to each individual horse, which was much more relationship based. The horses were coming along fantastically for me, but it was based on my reactions to them in each moment rather than any actual education they were receiving. So basically, we were learning how to relate to each other rather than their learning specific cues that would then be transferable to other riders. Loving people with good relationship skills ended up enjoying horses they purchased from me immensely. People who just wanted to ride and didn't care about the horse's opinion—well, they typically got hurt, resulting in an angry phone call to me at some point. I had no idea what I was doing wrong, because what I was experiencing with the horses I was training was better than anything I had done up until that point. It felt awesome, they were willing, and I was able to do more than ever before, including an epic ride on Dusty without any equipment on him whatsoever.

Some things seemed like they were beginning to fall apart. My new love and I had to move because being with me meant a divorce for her and losing the property we were living on. Nothing was going smoothly with my business, and I couldn't wrap my head around the training issues other people were experiencing with my horses. We needed money desperately, so we made a huge decision to sell off all the horses except two, one for each of us, and move back to my hometown, where I would return to my job at the pawnshop while we got our lives in order and decided what we wanted for our future.

It was a scary time, but we found a cute little house with some land; and even though we had no idea what was in store, we were excited to be really starting our lives over, together and completely, ridiculously in love.

EIGHT

-You Can't Really Sell Your Soul-

*"Integrity is exhibited not in thought, verbal promise,
or contract—only in action."*
~ M. Chandler McLay

[It took less than two weeks to get a contract on you after placing you up for sale. A wealthy man from Louisville was flying in to ride you for a second time and give me a down payment before scheduling your trailer ride to Kentucky. I was a little sad for you to leave, but it was just business as usual—except usually, with the others I mean, I hadn't spent a year dedicating time to them every day and developing the kind of trust and relationship that you and I had. You had carried me safely through every situation I dared take you into, and I was definitely going to miss having such a reliable partner to ride through the storms of my life.

Your buyer was so impressed, as of course he should have been. You were magnificent. At just coming up on three years of age, you had hundreds of miles of experience in all kinds of environments, and absolutely anyone could ride you. He even asked me if you were drugged the first time he met you—he asked again when I forgot to cinch the saddle tight enough and it ended up clinging to your belly as you walked around without a care in the world. You were my pride and joy, and at that point in my life, I had no greater accomplishment than you. You gave my life purpose, and I adored you.

As I stood in the field after loading you up for your big journey, everything seemed OK. Everything seemed OK, right up until you began to roll away, and you called out to me. You turned around and looked at me from the opening in the trailer door, and you called to me, over and over again, as the truck and trailer carried you further down the driveway to the gate and out onto the road ahead. You screamed for me, relentlessly, all the way down the drive and out the gate, and you continued to call for me down the entire stretch of highway that ran alongside the 25-acre property where we lived. Everything was obviously not OK.

I stumbled back up the long path to our house, falling repeatedly, as tears streamed down my face and blocked my view. I sobbed over what I had just done; my body wrenched in aching pain. Something broke inside of me that would never be fully healed. I had just sold the one horse I had ever allowed myself to fully trust, or really

love. My soul apparently had a price tag, and that tag read "Dusty -
$6,500 FIRM."}

+++++++++++++

Selling Dusty, combined with all the confusion I was experiencing as a horse trainer learning that a relationship was simply not transferable, left me hollow inside. I surrendered to life once again and took my old job back in my hometown, trying to put all my focus on repairing the wounds and financial damage of a life full of bad relationships and decisions. I needed structure, and structure is what I got that year.

We were able to buy a nice little house with an acre of land for the two horses we decided to keep. We had no intention of doing much with them any time soon, but our love of riding horses is what brought Brandy and me together, and we knew that in time it would become our shared passion again. We kept our two American Paint Horse mares, Honey and Velvet. Both were products of my horse trading days. I had purchased Honey from a place in deep, south Texas for a mere $500, which was a great deal at that time for a registered, flashy, buckskin Paint filly. I couldn't even think of selling her once my love was attached to her. Honey and Velvet were a great match for one another. I had originally brokered Velvet for the ranch, a little over a year before. She was the result of a trade I had made, swapping a pony mare I had in training for a four-year-old Velvet. I only had $400 invested in the pony, so it was a great trade. I trained up Velvet at the ranch. She was a pretty, jet-black, breeding-stock mare, and I sold her as a trail horse for $1,600. Just after selling Dusty, I received a call from the woman who had purchased Velvet, asking if I could help her sell Velvet. Her daughter was no longer interested, and Velvet had become difficult to work with. The woman wanted more money than she had paid for Velvet, and it was clear through our conversations that her training wasn't near what it had been a year previously. I told her I didn't know if I could get that price for her, but I'd at least come help her with trailer loading and such. I showed up and was stunned by the horse's beauty. She had matured and become an absolutely gorgeous mare. Heartbroken over losing Dusty, I offered her the asking price so long as I could pay it out monthly. She accepted, and I paid $1,800 for a horse I originally had invested $400 in—my horse-trading days were officially over.

Life got busy with having a regular job and a fixed schedule and building a new life with my love. We traveled a lot, found the structure we had been seeking, and repaired the financial mess of our previous relationships. We spent time loving on our horse girls, but we were too busy to ride; and quite frankly, the longer we didn't ride, the more nervous we became about starting up again. We cleaned up their pasture every day and talked to them. It was the first time I had ever spent time with horses this way, just caring for them with no agenda. It was so strange to me to go from being in the saddle every single day to not climbing on a horse's back for nearly a year. We could barely afford to feed them and attend to their other needs, and we stressed many times over whether or not it made any sense to keep horses that we weren't even riding. It was so deeply ingrained in us that horses were a waste of money unless they were earning their keep.

My education, experience, and new sensitivity made working at the pawn shop an impossible environment for me to thrive in. My boss and I could not see eye to eye, and we were arguing a lot. He damn near fired me on the spot when I gave him my two weeks' notice, and when I surprised everyone by showing up the next day, he took me downstairs and offered me a better position at higher pay. I declined and took a new job in an office at a big box retail home improvement store. Apparently I needed to fly my new rainbow flag a little higher and become a stereotype. I cut my hair short that year too, and I changed my name.

That job provided just what I needed to maintain the structure I was creating and to get our personal business in order. It also allowed me to start up research on how I might be able to get back into horses professionally in a way that felt good again. The first big news I came across was that the famous Aussie trainer who had heavily influenced my training methods was moving to Texas! Not just Texas, though, but the actual town where I went to college, which was just a short trip down the highway from where we lived. Coincidentally, one of his famous competitors had just made my hometown his new home as well. I was being surrounded by masters of the Natural Horsemanship movement, and I was sure this was a sign that new possibilities were in my near future. When I read that my DVD mentor was taking applications for his newly relocated company, I immediately applied. I heard back from them the very next day to schedule my interview. I was beyond excited.

It was my first major interview, and though I was incredibly nervous, I was also confident because I knew this guy's work inside and out and had successfully applied it in my own work on many occasions. I was a huge fan, and I just knew I would be an asset to them. I was applying to work within the actual business, not as a horse trainer; I still wasn't convinced I belonged in the professional saddle. When I didn't get the job, I was absolutely devastated, and I wanted to know why they had denied me. I wanted to prove myself to them and try to earn another shot, so I applied to volunteer at his next local tour stop, and I was accepted for that. I spent that weekend working for and with all the people who had gotten the job I wanted. I asked them lots of questions, and I found out that they all had one thing in common—no working knowledge of who this guy was or what he really did before they were specifically trained on the language he wanted them to use to sell his program and products. They were essentially robots with no agenda about horses themselves. Ah. Now it made sense. I would have been a horrible choice for them indeed. Looking back, what I should have looked up to him for was the way he did business, not the way he handled horses.

I realized what a blessing that denial had been and that I had no interest at all in working for someone else in that capacity. I wanted to make a name for myself. I wanted it to be my name that people associated with having success with horses. I was more motivated than ever to find my place in the professional horse world, and I went back to my office job to figure out how to do just that.

Not too long after, that same trainer did a segment on his television series with Pete Ramey—a natural hoof care practitioner from Georgia, or what people in our area referred to as "one of those barefoot weirdoes." Up until that point, I hadn't really known what to do about our horses' hooves. We just had them trimmed by a friend because I didn't know much about hoof care or what was needed, and we weren't doing anything with the horses anyway, so it didn't seem to be a concern. I watched the natural hoof care show with great interest, and it made a lot of sense to me. I learned many ways their health could be improved by using this method, and if it was good enough for a famous trainer that I admired, it was good enough for us to try. We hired the closest certified barefoot trimmer I could find, 90 miles away, and our whole world of horses began to change.

The barefoot movement was especially controversial at the time. It could take time to produce results, it required a holistic understanding of the horse's health, and it generally put the horse's welfare before anyone's use of them. It was very confrontational for horse owners who wanted to just slap a horseshoe on and get to work or play. I was engulfed in learning. It was so fascinating, bringing the science of horses into the equation in a way that made so much sense. We were seeing a vast improvement in our horses' health and well-being. They were happier, healthier, and more fun to be around than ever before. I wish I had had the good sense to make the connection that we had also been off their backs for a year, only spending quality time with them, but no—I attributed all the new goodness to their amazing new hoof regimen and the diet and management that came with its understanding.

The only problem was that we could barely afford the horses as it was, and the new hoof care was really expensive for us. I decided I would learn to trim the horses myself, so we could save that money. I looked up Pete Ramey online and discovered he was taking some time off from teaching. I was disappointed, but I just moved on to whom he recommended to learn from instead. I chose a woman in Illinois and signed up for my first class at her home. She was a brilliant teacher, and she encouraged me to consider becoming a professional by the end of our first workshop together. I was really resistant at first because a relationship with horses was my passion, but when I learned how much I could make as a trimmer, I figured that it was a much better way to sustain myself than working at some home improvement warehouse office. Plus, it got me that much closer to what I really wanted to be doing, and at least I'd be in the horse industry again. Besides, I'd be running my own business again, setting my own schedule, and having the flexibility that my life had been really missing. Even then, however, I knew I only wanted professional hoof care to be a stepping stone on my path.

I spent about a year taking classes and mentoring through trips back and forth to Illinois, photos, and endless emails and conversations. I practiced on any horse I could get my hands on. I would trim for co-workers at a reduced rate. In conversations with my first clients, they learned that I could train horses as well. A couple of them asked me to start their horses under saddle for them. Before I knew what was happening, I was trimming and training horses and moving quickly out of my regular job and back into the professional world of horses.

I had learned a great deal during my training hiatus, and it was serving me very well now. The same year I began trimming professionally, I picked up my first spiritual text outside of a religious context. It was through reading it, while sitting on a plane one afternoon and contemplating the world below me, that I was introduced to the universal nature of life. As I flipped through the first book of my conscious spiritual journey, I began to cry uncontrollably, trying desperately to keep from disturbing the people around me. After growing up in a Southern Baptist church and being constantly bombarded with conflicting ideas and information, I was finally being introduced to the concepts of love and life in ways that actually made sense to me. I don't mention the particular book that opened me up because it isn't one I would recommend today, but it was the doorway for me at the time. It was then—the first of many epiphanies I would have at 30,000 feet over the next several years—that I felt a power within me that until that point had been completely derived from things and others outside myself. I got the very first glimpse of who I really was and what I was capable of doing in this life. I could create my own experience. I had had all the control I ever needed, all along.

NINE

-No Bits, No Spurs, No Shoes-

*"Change is the essence of life; be willing to surrender what
you are for what you could become."*
~ Reinhold Niebuhr

{You were the promise of a mend to my broken heart. For some stupid reason I believed that if I did right by you, it would somehow heal the wound of selling your brother. You were his full sibling, two years his junior, and your coat was the one color I could never turn away—buckskin. I figured your deeply tan body would keep me from thinking of him, but knowing you were his genetic match would keep him alive in my heart.

I started you on my own terms, using all that I had learned in the three years since graduating college. No metal would ever touch your body. By this time, I could start colts with my eyes closed without worrying about much, and on your first ride outside of the round pen, you were riding among much more seasoned horses across 20,000 acres of grasslands in only a halter. When someone would have trouble with one of their horses on the trail, I would offer your back to them without telling them your age, and you would keep them safe while I worked out any issues with their own, more experienced horses. I was so proud of you. There was just one problem.

At the age of three, something horrible happened. Something went wrong in your genetic profile, and the buckskin faded away within months to grey. How could it be? Even your breeder didn't believe me until I sent her photos. You had turned into a carbon copy of your brother, Dusty. I could barely even catch myself or stop myself from calling you his name after that. It was more than I could stand. Every time I looked at you, Tucker, I hated myself. So what was my solution? I sold you—much more selectively than your brother and to someone who became a much-needed close friend for a while, but I sold you nonetheless. Some lessons have to be repeated before the learning really sets in. You were the last of my horses to ever be sold.}

+++++++++++++

A lot happened during my last year at the big blue box. I became a dedicated student of the horse, especially where the hooves were concerned. I also became a student of understanding life. In my little corner of the office and in between my responsibilities at work, I was studying every book I could get my hands on in regard to the current science behind holistic horse care. I had a lot to catch up on as the word "holistic" was pretty new to my vocabulary in and of itself. If my head got too full of horses, I'd switch to books on mastering life and understanding my spirituality, which was definitely a new endeavor as well. It was during that time that the two worlds came together for me one afternoon and set my course for a destination I never imagined.

On the personal side of things, I had learned through my reading that in order for me to get what I wanted out of life, I had to decide what that was. I had to set an intention. I needed a purpose for being here. I had always thought that that was one of those things you were supposed to figure out, as if it were a secret buried deep within you already, which is what keeps a lot of people from ever moving forward. In actuality, the part about it being within you already is true, but it's no secret. The beauty of human nature is that we have the free will to choose what we came here to do, even if at a soul level we already know. It is in making the choice that the "secret" is discovered, because the part of us that knows what we want is the part that has been trying to guide us all along. Most of us are just too busy listening to everyone else to hear it. I knew at this point that my life was about something much larger than horses, but for some reason I was being called to partner with them in whatever I was here to do. Just saying that or acknowledging it at that time in my life was scary. I was just barely being introduced to—or remembering about, you might say—"going within" or listening to my body in order to use my feelings as indicators of truth in my life.

I was having a hard time putting this so-called purpose into words, and I had read somewhere that when the words finally came out, if they were on target, it was common to become overwhelmed with emotion. I was sitting at my desk one afternoon, reading one of the most important books I had gotten my hands on to date—*The Soul of a Horse* by Joe Camp—when suddenly, the words popped into my head. I slammed the book down and grabbed a pen, and I quickly scribbled the message, "My purpose is to raise human consciousness and inspire love through my experiences with and knowledge of horses." My arms and legs were covered in goose bumps, and tears came down my face despite my best efforts to stop them. I had no idea where this message was going to take me, but I knew that if I just kept moving forward in alignment with this statement, my life was going to make sense, and everything would turn out OK. What I didn't plan on was the hailstorm the universe was about to slam into me in order for me to grow and realize what "raise consciousness" meant.

See, I figured it was somewhere along the lines of "since I knew so much, and everyone else knew so little, I needed to be the one to inform them and help them pull their heads out of their asses." As it turns out, that's the kind of thinking that goes with having your head up your own ass in the first place. It also means I wasn't very spiritually conscious at all—I just knew how to retain information. I don't even know how to bring all of the factors together to explain just how cocky I had become at this time in my life. I had everything going for me in the eyes of a lot of people, including myself. My finances were in order, and I was making good money and using my free time to learn what I really wanted to do, and I was already doing it. I was happy and committed in love to an amazing, supportive, and stunningly beautiful woman, which also got me a lot of attention. Other beautiful women began noticing me as well. I had my dream truck, a Harley Davidson; I was a homeowner; and I had a huge circle of friends who wanted to hang out all the time. At work, I was extremely popular with both my co-workers and my managers. People trusted me. I knew everything that was going on behind the scenes in our store, and I had more autonomy than necessary because of that. After the shitty experience I had in high school, this felt like the high school experience all over again, except that I was an overly confident mix between the homecoming queen and the star quarterback this time around. Considering what I was beginning to learn in the books I was studying, it was kind of ironic that it was leading me into a situation where my ego was absolutely out of control. However, it was because of what I was learning that I was able to actually see what I was doing even while I was doing it, and that was definitely new to me. I became absolutely disgusted with my behavior on more than one occasion.

My perfect little world came crashing down within a few months of running wild with my faulty new understanding of my power as a human being. After officially quitting my regular job to run my new hoof care business full time, I slipped into a dark place of fear, self-loathing, and unworthiness. I had enough work to feel hopeful, but because of the nature of the direction I was taking with horses, and living in Texas of all places, I had very little support or belief in what I was trying to do. Very few people back then believed most horses could go without shoes, and some of the things I was suggesting about horse training were even harder for them to swallow. My parents were afraid because I had left a secure job. Everyone I knew in the horse industry was beginning to look at with me with some curiosity, but mostly it looked more like they thought I was losing my mind as I moved further and further away from traditional thinking around horses. My co-workers sneered and jokingly said I would be back in a few months when my business failed, projecting their own insecurities upon me. Brandy, my hoof care mentor, and the few clients I already had were my only real supporters at the time. I freaked out thinking I was going to fail, and I started partying for the first time in my life. It was how I coped through the scariest three months while I developed my business.

I had skipped that whole part in high school and college where you went out dancing and drinking and had cool parties, which was pretty obvious by my tolerance—or lack thereof—for alcohol. For three months, if I wasn't out working, I was hosting some of the wildest, drunken, all-girl parties you can imagine. I always took photos so that I could look the next day and see what had happened, because I definitely didn't remember. Those photo review sessions were always filled with giggles, gasps, and embarrassment to say the least. I could say that I deeply regret that time in my life, but I actually don't. It was really fun when it was fun, and it was really awful when I made decisions that hurt myself and others, and I learned a great deal. I experienced maybe the deepest depression of my lifetime during those months, when my own limited understanding of healthy relationships combined with my outrageous arrogance caused me to lose a friend I had grown to love very deeply. It was the first time I was really painfully broken open in a life-changing way.

After a few weeks of considering it a major achievement to get from my bed into the bathtub without drowning myself, my business started picking up, and I began to heal from my bad decision making. I may have been sabotaging my personal life in a great many ways, but where the horses were concerned, I was really doing well. My background in horse training coupled with my business degree set me up for real success as a hoof care provider. I was good with the people, great with the horses, and good at the work itself, and I always showed up on time and maintained a tight schedule. Within just a few short months, I had doubled the income I was making at my previous job, and life was looking really exciting. However, as passionate as I was about horse care, it was working with horses on a relationship basis that I was really missing, so I put just as much focus into that part of my life again.

I had been starting colts all during this time, both for myself and a few other people. If the horse had any previous training, I didn't want to deal with it. I was learning a lot from the horses by having a clean slate to work with during their training. The most significant thing I learned during this time was the irrelevance of the use of bits in the horses' mouths. I had always started young horses in just a halter and then moved to the bit to finish them out. However, with my skills far more developed than they had been in the past, I began to question the validity of a bit in the first place since every horse I was training was performing exactly as I asked without the metal in their mouths. We usually didn't run into problems until the first time I would try to use a bit with each horse. When I brought this up with others in the horse world, I was looked at like a crazy person. I even tried to ask famous trainers who were known for bridleless demonstrations in the arena, and I was still met with alarm at the suggestion of not using a bit.

I was so frustrated by this. I had become quite confident in my horse-training abilities by now, to the point that I didn't care if everyone else thought I was crazy. Being in an openly romantic relationship with another woman had already given me strength against the masses. Going into natural hoof care, led by others who had already succeeded in that field, strengthened me further. My gut said that bits were bad news for horses, and I was finally at a place in my life where I had the strength and courage to trust that, so I ditched them in my training.

I didn't tell my clients at first. They wouldn't hear it. I just trained the horses, and when the client arrived to take their freshly started horse on their first trail ride together, I'd ask them to hop on with just the rope halter in place. When it was questioned, I simply asked them to please just trust me and try it. Every single time they were blown away by the results. The horse did everything they asked, without a bit. After this was the consistent result each time I started a horse, I got rid of the last two bits in my tack room and swore I would never use one again. It felt wrong to put metal in a horse's mouth, and it got me questioning a lot of things, especially about how often pain or the threat of pain was the primary component of getting a horse to do what you wanted.

It didn't take long for me to find out that I wasn't the only one questioning things—not by a long shot. I was excited to learn that many people, much older and more experienced than I in a lot of ways, were beginning to speak out for the horse, and people were beginning to listen. Joe Camp was one of these people, and his books made a huge impact in the horse world. He was the first I know of to give horse owners permission to question the status quo and trust their feelings more. He did a ton of research and published some very important information in his first two horse books, *The Soul of a Horse* and its sequel. I began giving out copies of this book to anyone I was training for, and I required they read it before showing up for their first lesson with their horse. Those books were confirmation that I wasn't crazy and that I wasn't the only one thinking this way. They also led me even further down the rabbit hole, a hole I'm still traveling down today.

Mark Rashid was another heavy influence on me at the time. His books taught me two very important lessons concerning horses and also confirmed some thoughts I had been having concerning herd dynamics and leadership. First, he introduced me to the concept of passive leadership rather than dominance-based leadership. Most of Natural Horsemanship is based on following the model of the dominant horse in the herd's behavior toward other horses in order to get results. Mark's model came through observations looking not for control of others but relationship amongst horses. He found that the true leaders of the herd were the horses that had the most friends, the ones that were most balanced in their behavior and not as aggressive as the so-called dominant horse. I had witnessed this in my own herd and believed it to be absolutely true. I stopped bossing my horses around for this very reason and began to seek cooperation instead. That's not the most important thing I learned from Mark, though.

Mark's books were the first I had come across to discuss the idea that the horse is never wrong. The first time I read those words, I understood them immediately; and in everything I have ever learned about horses, and later where it concerns the rest of life and interactions with other beings, there are not many statements more true than this one. Basically, it means that given what the horse understands from his unique perspective, it is never in a trainer's best interest to make the horse wrong for not understanding what you want from him. I immediately applied this to my own training methods, and the results were incredible. I adopted this principle as one of my absolute beliefs when it came to working with horses, and I had no idea just how relevant it would remain in my life. Under this concept, fighting with horses became a thing of the past, and understanding combined with cooperation became my new reality.

My horse training began evolving at lightning speed because it was being combined with my scientific understanding of horses through my holistic studies in hoof care and management. My spiritual path was evolving as well as I introduced more books filled with wisdom that offered even greater insight into my pursuits with horses and my interactions with people. The struggle then became the disconnect between what I was learning and experiencing with horses on a daily basis and the reality of where most of the rest of the world was in their own understanding of horses, as a society in general. Slowly, it was becoming apparent that we humans, around the globe, had horses all wrong.

TEN

-High Hopes-

"Excellence is the Result of Caring more than others think is Wise, Risking more than others think is Safe, Dreaming more than others think is Practical, and Expecting more than others think is Possible."
~ Ronnie Oldham

{After so much time off your back, I was afraid you wouldn't listen to me the first time I climbed back on. I had little to prepare me for what happened instead. In the safety of our little pasture, I swung up on your strong, shiny, black back and asked you to move out—only, I didn't put anything on your face to control you. There was nothing between me and you besides the connection I prayed would be there after all this time. I had never attempted to ride you this way before, and I didn't know why I felt inclined to try that day.

My mouth was probably gaping open in astonishment as you carried me around the pasture, changing directions, stopping, and backing with nothing more than subtle cues from my body. I had not trained you to do this. Sure, they were the same cues I had used to train you with equipment, but you didn't have equipment on now, and you obviously knew that. You listened to me anyway. This broke every rule I knew to be true about horse training, especially since you had not ever received any repetitive or consistent training to prepare you for such things, and I hadn't ridden you in over a year.

I wanted to see just how far we could test these new waters, so I loaded you up and took you to a dear friend who had a large obstacle course in her pasture. Everyone smiled when I unloaded you with just a neck rope and headed out to the obstacles. You performed beyond my wildest expectations, carrying me through the poles at a trot, backing through and around corners, going over the see-saw, and then jumping up and then down off the big platform. Even when I lost my balance a bit, leaning too far forward and hitting my chin on the back of your head during the downward jump, you were right there with me. I got dizzy and started to lose my seat; you steadied yourself and caught me.

I had no explanation for what had just happened, but now I was hungrier than I had ever been to understand my relationship to you. I hadn't ridden you in over a year, and you definitely hadn't ridden like that, even with equipment, the last time I sat on your back. You had just given me a real taste of my dream to ride in total freedom. You had just disproven so much I previously understood to be true. Velvet—you had just unlocked Pandora's Box.}

+++++++++++++

In my first year of trimming professionally, I received an invitation that would skyrocket my learning in every area of my life. I was asked by another hoof care professional to join him and about ten others in a meeting of holistic horse care professionals and advocates to discuss how we might better be able to reach out and educate the public about our various areas of expertise and study. I was scared to go. I did not think I belonged in such a group because I was just beginning to learn about many of these topics, and I was afraid I wouldn't have much to contribute. One of my friends and clients at the time encouraged me to go anyway, and it was her urging combined with my gut screaming how much I would regret it if I didn't that ultimately made me decide to go. I was so nervous, and I was the youngest person there by a long shot.

This gathering had included some well-known hoof care people around Texas, including a woman who was considered one of the people responsible for bringing natural hoof care to America in the first place. There was also a horse trainer and feed developer from Australia who would become one of my greatest teachers. I was in total awe of him. Not only was he a bitless and barefoot advocate, completely against the use of any metal against the horse for any reason, but he had also developed a brilliant and scientifically based feed for horses that produced some pretty amazing results. That wasn't what hooked me on him, though. During his time to share, he told us the story of his farewell to his native land before making America his home. Before leaving Australia, he took his daughter's horse on a magnificent journey of many days down the coastline, completely bridleless and bareback the entire way. My heart probably stopped when I heard this story. He had just described my wildest fantasy, a dream that I only believed to be possible in my head, which I had never uttered out loud.

Up until that point, the idea most people had of bridleless riding consisted of the now famous rides performed in reining competitions inside an arena. I admit—the first time I saw a woman ride like that on a beautiful, black horse I was just as excited as everyone else. However, I had learned the truth of such situations through my experiences as a trainer. Those horses were so conditioned through repetition that being bridleless was simply for show. It wasn't real, and it wasn't indicative of the relationship between the horse and rider. It was the same exact reason a person could turn a seasoned barrel horse loose into an arena with the barrels set up, and the horse would run the pattern by itself, without a rider even on board. That's not to say there was no relationship between those horses and their riders; it just means that their not having equipment on their heads didn't prove anything in those particular situations, and you didn't see those same horses out on open public trails like that. My dream was to prove that horses could in fact be ridden without equipment, in every situation, through mastery of your relationship with them, and this guy had just told me that it wasn't merely a pipe dream I had. It was true, and he had done it. My mare proved it to me as well, very soon after.

That was just part of what I came away with that life-changing day. Our hosts for this gathering were three incredible women—one in particular, but all guardians and stewards of an amazing ranch in the North Texas Hill Country. I had never knowingly come into contact with human beings quite like this before. Each in their own way, they were like medicine women, and I found it hard to pay attention to the conversation at times because I was too busy being affected by their presence. They embodied wisdom and a stillness I had never directly experienced in another human before, and definitely not in myself. I didn't know what magic they possessed, but I knew I desperately needed it in my own life, and I wanted to know them.

I had to leave the meeting early that day to get to a hoof care appointment, so I missed the chance to speak to any of them. I was very drawn to one of these women specifically that day, and as I was driving away from this new circle of friends, I felt something urging me to turn around. From the driver's seat of my truck, I turned and found her staring right back at me, almost into me. It was as if something had been exchanged between us, as if a yearning to connect was mutually felt. I almost felt as if we had just had a brief unspoken conversation that we would meet again very soon. I had never experienced anything like this, but I had been reading about such things, and I just shook my head and smiled because the concepts I was beginning to know as truth in my life were unfolding right before my eyes.

We did make contact very soon after, and I arranged for Brandy and me to bring our horses out to the ranch to stay the night and ride. It was a magical weekend. I spent a little time getting to know these women, but I especially got to know the one I had connected with at the end of the previous gathering. She had a young mare she wanted started under saddle, and I had a thirst for knowledge in many of the areas she had an understanding of, so we worked out a wonderful trade arrangement, and my life began to transform. I was introduced to many areas of spiritual tradition through the ranch, but for the time being most of my new learning came in the form of nutrition and counseling to uncover some of the blocks in my relationship to myself. I knew one thing for sure—I wanted to be a part of the magic of this place. That opportunity came about a year later, and my love and I joined the many others around the globe that consider this ranch a place of safety and refuge, a home away from home for those who are passionate about creating a kinder, gentler world.

ELEVEN

-The Path Is Revealed-

*"All truth passes through three stages. First, it is ridiculed.
Second, it is violently opposed. Third, it is accepted as
being self-evident."*
~ Arthur Schopenhauer

{I received the call about you late one evening. The woman on the other line sounded like she was in pain and uncertain about what to do. You were hurting, and the thought of losing you had her seeking answers outside of her comfort zone. Someone had told her I might be able to help you, but she wasn't sure.

Your hooves were on fire, and it was hard for you to stand. I wasn't very experienced; you were the first acute founder case to find its way to me, but I was ready. I told her with confidence that I could help you, but she would have to trust me and follow my instructions exactly. You were so beautiful, an absolute dream horse of my earlier days, and I was determined to save your life.

A few weeks later, after the X-rays revealed 12-to-15-degree rotations of the coffin bones in each of your front hooves, she was losing hope. The veterinarians she had spoken with had given you a death sentence, telling her your pain level was too great and that it would be kinder to put you down. She hadn't given me enough time. I could still help you. She called me in tears to tell me of her decision to follow their advice and let you go. I begged her to turn you over to me, to let me take you home. You would become mine, and I would heal you. She said yes.

I showed up the next morning nervous but confident I could keep my promise to both her and you. After a few weeks at home with me, a subsolar abscess in each front hoof revealed the tips of your coffin bones. I was terrified, but you were still improving, and your comfort level was reasonable. More weeks went by, and my meticulous care of your hooves and management was beginning to pay off. You could walk comfortably without your therapeutic boots. Then I was able to turn you out with the other horses. The day finally arrived when I felt it was time to get a new follow-up with a different vet.

The new X-rays showed no rotation. We had done it! In eight months, you and I were able to grow a new set of hooves that proved the experts wrong. Your results and story were published. I retrained you using much softer methods than your roping horse days, and you taught so many people about riding without bits. You also did it on hooves that had previously sentenced you to death and were now stomping across rocky terrain without any pain. You changed the world of every person that met and experienced you. You told me your name even before I was ready or willing to listen, and now, Travis, I will protect you and keep you safe for the rest of your life.}

+++++++++++++

All I wanted to do was learn more about relationships with horses and what was possible when they were the focus of training, but by this time, I had become quite a popular little hoof trimmer. My people, business, and horse skills combined made for a very successful skill set, and by my second year of trimming professionally, I couldn't take on any more clients. I was trimming 15 to 17 horses a day on average, and that was great, but this was never what I wanted to ultimately end up doing with my life. I don't say that without gratitude for everything that came with it, and as it usually turns out in life, my not being able to do what I really thought I wanted kept me from making a huge mistake.

I kept in contact with the feed developer I had met at the ranch gathering, but I did not have time to mentor under him. Instead, I suggested to one of my friends that she should check him out, and she ended up being his next protégé for a while. I was a little envious, but I had to focus on my business for the time being, and I was helping a lot of horses doing what I was already doing. I would get back to training at some point, and I could live vicariously through them for now. Still, I would check in as often as possible to learn as much as I could along the way, and I was applying anything I found interesting to my own horses and the horses I was training at home.

We had also stayed in close contact with the ladies at the ranch, and within about a year, we shared our desire to live nearby and work with horses there and in partnership with them. The universe must have been listening because they called back

the very next day to let us know that one of their rental proper-
ties, a few miles down the road, had suddenly become available.
We didn't even hesitate, and once again, we left my hometown to
set off on a new adventure. Everything was beginning to fall into
place. Brandy and I moved into a beautiful old farm house, and
I began to refocus on training and lessening the demands on me
for hoof care.

I had been telling all of my clients about this Australian guy
and the magic he did with horses. I had also started selling his
feed. Since I couldn't work with him directly, I offered to host a
clinic for him at the ranch, where I would be able to be a par-
ticipant. I was so sold on his methods and words, just as I had
been with all of the people who came before him who seemed to
know so much more than I did. During the clinic, though, one
of the participants who happened to be one of my hoof care clients was mumbling angrily to herself during one of his demonstrations. Initially, I was defensive toward her for challenging
this guy. He had done what I knew no one else to be able to
do, but part of me couldn't help hearing what she was saying
and agreeing. Here he was claiming that the key to a relationship and understanding with horses was to eliminate stress and
not ever cause them pain, yet we were required to work them in
knotted rope halters and run them in round pens, and the work
was meant to be repeated frequently. So much of what he said
made total sense, and I learned a great deal about the science
of horses from this man, but she was right. It was a direct contradiction in action to what he was saying out loud. One of the
great patterns in my life had been revealed, but it would take a
bit longer for me to see it for myself.

The horse I had taken to this clinic was my greatest challenge to date. He came with the name "Norman Bates." I
decided that was counterproductive to who I believed he could
be, so I changed his name to Harmony. Harmony, combined
with all of the questions now circling in my head about what

was actually true about horse training, caused a major shift. He was a dangerous horse when I first got him. He had been picked up by animal control, roaming the streets as a stallion. He was at least ten years old, very aggressive toward people, and downright angry. He reminded me of the stallion in the movie Buck, but I certainly didn't kill him. Instead, I listened to him. Nothing I knew as a trainer worked with him, but when I didn't back down or make demands, we got results. I began to invite people out to watch me work with him every Sunday because I was so blown away by what was happening, and I wanted people to witness it. I had no idea how to explain what was going on between me and this horse, but the audience gave me a way to reflect what I was experiencing, and it also gave me a chance to develop the public skills I would eventually need when I became the well-known clinician and trainer I wanted to be.

None of my training methods were working. I could move his feet all day long, and he would never give in. If I talked to him, though, and just unassumingly tried to figure him out, he would always allow me to approach him and get to work. I had worked with him this way about eight times before taking him to the clinic, and so much of what I had experienced with him beforehand was contradicted in what we were being taught that weekend. At one point, the clinician actually cast me aside and took over with my horse as he reprimanded me in front of the crowd, trying to take me down a notch in my self-righteousness. He wasn't able to get any better results with Harmony. I was so confused, but I was being forced to really weigh my own experiences against those belonging to people whose knowledge and experience I trusted. It was a really important lesson for me, especially considering what was coming next.

I spent a bit of time just experimenting with the horses I was currently working with. Forget going bitless—all I was interested in at that point was losing the bridle entirely and working with nothing more than a neck rope. That isn't a new concept in the horse world, at least as a training demonstration, but most horses are conditioned down to a neck rope, not ridden that way initially, and you never saw that kind of riding out on the trail. That's what I wanted to do. I knew it was possible, and I wanted people to experience what I had by not trying to control the horse's head. It was such a different level of freedom and a demonstration that the relationship between you and the horse was solid. I was convinced that it was our relationship that allowed us to ride horses in a kind and gentle way, not through training.

So much science was being published around this time to reveal the harm of using bits and shoes on horses. I was thrilled to have books and articles on the subject, written by people with the right credentials who had the audience to create some serious change. The more evidence that existed to show what we were actually doing to get horses to behave for us, the better the chances for a kinder world for the horses and better relationships between us and them. This is also about the time that I fell deeply into the self-righteous trap of right vs. wrong.

I defined truth a bit differently in those days. Back then, truth was based on facts, and facts were absolute. If you were causing harm to horses, you were wrong and needed to do something differently, in my opinion. It seems so stupid now, considering all the harm I was causing unknowingly. I lost a lot of friends and clients during those days, because even if someone could agree with what I was saying, not very many people wanted to due to how it was presented. With me as the authority and their being made to feel wrong, was I just blind to what should have been obvious—this was exactly what I knew not to do with horses when I wanted them to do something different?

One day, one of the ranch ladies put a DVD in my hand that would flip my world upside down. It was a documentary entitled *The Path of the Horse*. I recognized the first name in the list of trainers interviewed for the film. It was Mark Rashid, who at the time was my favorite of the famous trainers I knew of. I didn't know any of the others, two of them being foreign. I took the film home and sat down to what would turn out to be one of the most influential hours of my life.

TWELVE

-Breaking Free-

"Maybe there's a way out of the cage where you live
Maybe one of these days you can let the light in
Show me how big your brave is"
~ Sara Bareilles

{I had met you only briefly three months before, but I realized then that you might just be the one to make my big dream come true. I needed permission from your guardian, of course, which she so graciously granted, after I proved I had the skill to pull off my desire for you.

I returned to visit you, and I could barely contain myself. I slipped my fancy new cordeo around your neck and climbed on your back. You carried me into the mountains, through rivers, and eventually down the coastline and into the waves, showing me some of the most beautiful country this planet has to offer. Locals and other visitors stared wide-eyed as I rode past them on the beautiful, and totally naked, white horse. Your only garments were a blue-and-black, custom-made rope that draped loosely around your neck, and the girl on your back whose smile was beginning to make her face hurt from its intensity.

My dream had come true. I was riding in absolute freedom, bareback and bridleless, in all types of unpredictable situations and terrain, in a foreign country, on a horse I barely knew. It was a task that had never been asked of you to such an extent before, and you were flawless. Everything I believed was possible became real that day. It was one of the absolute greatest moments I would ever experience on horseback, and I am so grateful to you for that gift. On the final stretch of beach, I shot my hands into the air and stared at the heavens, believing that life really could not get any better than what I had experienced that day. It was a rare experience of lasting happiness, and I could not stop smiling for days.

A month later, everything changed. I went back and looked at the pictures of us together on the beach that day, and I saw the truth. I saw a smiling, happy human on top of a compliant and beautiful white horse, whose eyes were often filled with discomfort and whose expression never matched mine. I saw the disconnect between my emotions and your own. I saw why it's so very important that a rider can only see the back of the horse's head and not his face.}

+++++++++++++

It would actually take about two years for me to humble down enough to seek guidance for what I had been exposed to in *The Path of the Horse*. On the one hand, I was thrilled and amazed to be introduced to the likes of Alexander Nevzorov at the end of the film. On the other, here was yet another master sure to let me down in some way. He had to be just like the others—filled with contradictions—but I couldn't get it out of my head what I had seen him doing with his horses. I listened to what others said about him, about the supposed rigidity and dogma of his school. They likened it to a cult. I decided I would just use him as proof that what I already believed could be done was true, and I would figure it out on my own.

My bridleless riding and training was going really well. I was able to ride more and more horses without equipment on their heads, and it was hard for anything else to compare to that feeling. However, I didn't have a horse I had started that way, so I always questioned the authenticity of the connection since all of them had, in fact, been ridden with equipment previously. It was astonishing to me how few people had any interest in riding without a bridle. I understood their fear, but what I didn't understand was that they could not see the contradiction between having a good relationship and needing equipment to control the horse. Didn't one cancel out the other? I no longer wanted to ride horses, knowing that the only reason I was getting to do what I wanted was because I had a piece of equipment to make it happen. I wanted a real relationship, I wanted connection, and I wanted what everyone claimed they had—a horse who WANTED to be ridden. I was on a mission to seek out truth in my life, and so far, the truth was hard to handle. The more I kept moving this direction with my training, though, the more amazing the results.

I went to a holistic horse symposium in St. Louis that year with several friends and my hoof care mentor. There, I met some really impressive people from around the world who were on the cutting edge of understanding the science of horses. Alexander Nevzorov was there also, at least his book was, and I told my friends not to waste their time. I had since learned that he no longer rode horses, and to be a part of his School, you had to give it up. Hell if I was going to stop riding after seeing the way he could ride. I wanted that for myself. I had decided the only way I was going to do what I really wanted was to start with a baby and train him bridleless, from start to finish. I didn't just want any horse, though; I wanted a stallion. I was really on the fence about breeding horses, but I was considering breeding my mare to get the colt I wanted, and I had already begun looking at studs for her. I'm not sure what I was thinking. Actually, I know exactly what I was thinking, and it was only about myself. Forget that I would artificially impregnate my horse with the semen of some other horse she hadn't even met—I only had a fifty-fifty chance at getting a colt anyway. The universe already had that one figured out, thankfully, but it would be a few more months before the answer came.

In the meantime, I had started stalking Nevzorov information online. I had watched all the videos I could find and found one of his representatives on Facebook. She and I began what turned into a year-long discussion leading to friendship. It was the no riding that I couldn't handle thinking about. I mean, without my riding ability, who was I anyway? We would dabble in the discussion of what the School had to offer, and then I'd run away to experiment on my own some more. I turned to studying one of the other trainers in the film instead, a man by the name of Klaus Ferdinand Hempfling.

Hempfling's philosophy really resonated with me, but there were photos of bits and shoes, and I had no way of being OK with that considering the education I had in the science surrounding those items and the harm they caused to the horse. Basically, if metal was being used on the horse in any way or rope halters with knots over pressure points, I could no longer buy into the notion that pain, or the threat of pain, wasn't being used to control the horse. Plus, a lot of the body language being used was just a subtle form of control that I was already experienced at. It was also really expensive to learn from Hempfling, whereas I had since learned that Nevzorov's school was free. That was a huge thing to consider. Honesty and integrity were what I was looking for, and I couldn't think of anything more honest than offering what you know for free. I was still a bit put off by other things, but more and more, all roads kept leading me back to Nevzorov.

I then turned to another book I had seen at the symposium in St. Louis—Michael Bevilacqua's *Beyond the Dream Horse*. That one really hit home. For the first time, I was seeing someone tell a story very similar to mine, including all the frustrations of a professional trainer in search of truth and the realization that a relationship could not be transferable. Being the world representative for Nevzorov Haute Ecole (NHE), he also painted a different picture of Alexander, and I finally realized how arrogant I was being to not even explore this a bit further. I decided to go ahead and read Alexander's book. It was mind-blowing, and it made a lot of sense to me. Confrontational and controversial for sure—but I was willing to put my ego away at least long enough to learn what I could from him. He had taken the leading science on horses and combined that with our history and relationship with them to make a very compelling argument against our modern use of horses. I still resisted joining the NHE School, though, because I didn't think I needed it, and I still wasn't considering giving up riding.

I also still wanted a stallion to train using the new methods I was learning so that I could partner with him and make a name for myself as a bridleless and liberty trainer. Nevzorov had a stallion—I had already picked a stud for Velvet, but I was open to considering other options. What I knew for sure was that I wanted a raw horse to start fresh with, one who had no previous training. The answer came the next morning in my e-mail, after a very powerful dream.

THIRTEEN

-The Death Card-

"Your breath touched my soul, and I saw beyond all limits."
~ Rumi

{I wasn't sure about you based on the photo and description I received. You were older than I wanted and a more elegant and refined breed than I had been hoping for. I went to meet you with an open mind, completely willing to walk away if you weren't the right one. None of that mattered, though. As soon as your eyes met mine, the fierce intensity of your soul burned right into mine, and that was it. In an instant, my fate was sealed, and the path I thought my life was taking took a wild turn. Half Egyptian Arabian, I decided to call you Shai, after the Egyptian god of fate and destiny. I bet you laughed at me with a knowing grin. You seemed to laugh at me a lot over the next several months.

You were skin and bone when we met, but you were not weak, and within weeks your body was muscular and shiny again. I had never seen a horse move quite like you before, as if gravity had to work twice as hard to keep you planted firmly on the ground. Every time I entered your world, my heart would race as your energy would explode all around me. Some days I wondered if I would ever be able to regain my composure or breathe normally in your midst. Nothing I had ever experienced on the back of a horse could quite compare to the adrenaline rush of being so close to your raw power on the ground. I had nothing to keep myself safe other than your perception of me in any given moment. More than once, you sent me away to learn how to be worthy of your presence.

I was hooked on you. I had worked with hundreds of horses, including stallions, but something was different about you. You weren't the first untrained horse I had ever been around, but you were the first that I had ever approached this way before, and that made all the difference. I realized very quickly something that would change everything. You were the first horse I had ever really met—including the 12 others in my pasture that I claimed to know so well—a free horse unencumbered by previous conditioning and under no restraint, without any emotional or physical pain to burden you. No history of abuse. Zero fear of humans. You were the purest form of who you really were, as if your soul was just as visible as your physical self.

You opened a door and offered a view of a truth that could never be unseen, and after you, there would be no going back.}

+++++++++++++

It was just another normal day, other than waking up shaken from a dream about a black and white stallion that morning. It was rare for me to have such vivid dreams, especially about something so current and with so much feeling involved. I sat down at my computer to check e-mails and immediately noticed one with an attachment that had the word "stallion" in the subject line. I instantly got one of those feelings when something seems far too obvious to be a coincidence. The e-mail was from a friend and client of mine in the Arabian horse circles. She knew I didn't want another horse but remembered my saying something about a stallion in my future. She wondered if I might consider one a little sooner as he was in dire need of help.

There was a breeding operation in North Texas where the owner had passed away, and the horses were left in their stalls with little to no care for weeks. No one in the extended family was interested in the horses, so instead they were basically left to starve or become someone else's problem. I guess I was going to become a someone else.

The first photo I received was of a stunning black and white Paint and Arabian cross. I immediately wanted him, but when I called to make the arrangements, he had already been spoken for. I was informed there was another stallion who still needed to be rescued, but he was a different breed. I was a little disappointed and also feeling a little silly for thinking too much along the lines of this situation being some sort of sign. However, when the second stallion's photo and information arrived, I was sure the synchronicity was not to be ignored. This guy was a black and white National Show Horse, an Egyptian Arabian and Saddlebred cross—exactly like the stud horse I had selected to eventually breed to my mare. I couldn't believe it. I was also relieved of the guilt for even considering bringing another baby animal into the world out of sheer selfish desire.

I was so excited. This was the horse who would help me achieve my big dream. I had only one goal left as a trainer, and I wanted to partner with this horse to publicly attain it. More than anything, I wanted to expose all of the information I had self-righteously come to know as lies in the horse industry. There were three parts to this goal. One was to prove to my little part of the world that horses could be trained start to finish without any means of coercion, control, or bribery and that I had the skill and understanding to do it. The second was to achieve for myself the relationship I believed, and had seen through Alexander Nevzorov, possible between a human and a horse. The third was to disprove most of the commonly held beliefs about horse behavior, care, training, and management in the Western world. It would only take a few short weeks to realize that the second reason would be all that ever really mattered.

When I met Shai, I knew he was the perfect match for my intention. I loaded him up and went right to work. I created a Facebook page for him and started a blog to keep track of our journey together, sharing the details with anyone interested. He would be the first horse I would attempt to work with in this way—with no body language, no ropes or sticks or even a halter, no rewards, no punishment, nothing at all other than my ability to show up and request what I wanted while being willing to walk away if he said no. At least, this was my interpretation of what was required to work with a horse the way Nevzorov did. I wasn't willing to join his school because I fully intended to ride my new horse, and I honestly believed that my experience and background had sufficiently prepared me without needing any additional help. Instead, I read everything I could get my hands on about their methods, and I vowed to follow the main principles, which I understood to be that I could never punish, get angry at, or harm Shai in any way and that I had to honor every "no" he gave me, no matter how subtle. Honoring his "no" by walking away was going to be the hardest challenge, given that that is the exact opposite of what anyone does as a horse trainer. I was willing to give it a go, however, because it was more about relationship now than training, and I no longer felt like being a horse trainer.

By the end of the first month with Shai, so much of what I had been taught was falling away to what my heart, and now my experience with this particular horse, knew to be true. Here is an excerpt taken from my Shai blog at week four:

> The most important lesson I've learned so far is this: The more control the human has in the training situation, the less the learning that takes place. Shai is teaching me things about myself, about horses, and about the level of communication possible between us in ways I never could have imagined.

> I'm not going to lie; he scares the shit out of me sometimes. He is so incredibly expressive and talkative. Sometimes I want to "protect" myself in the typical ways you are taught to be cautious with horses, but I just hold my breath and stay present. He hasn't attempted to hurt me yet, even though sometimes I misinterpret his body language or vocalizations for something less than friendly. This journey is requiring a lot of courage out of me. I've never really been around a stallion this much without any kind of restraint. He grunts and makes that special stallion nicker when he's excited, and sometimes it's over the oddest thing—like today when I was brushing his face. I get nervous and worry what his reaction is going to be, but so far, all I have to do is tell him no if I think he's about to cross the line, and it never goes there. Each day my belief that fear with horses is simply a lack of understanding is reinforced in a big way.

By week five, I was realizing just how dangerous this kind of work could get for someone who didn't have my kind of experience with horses, and I began getting nervous about sharing what I was doing publicly. I was scared someone would try to duplicate what I was doing without the same level of understanding and feel and that they would get badly hurt—especially if they went out and tried it with a stallion like I was doing. The deeper I got with Shai, the less it seemed appropriate for the public, for many reasons. The more I treated him like an equal, the more he became one, and the more I began to question my motives for exposing our developing relationship for my own personal gain. I was feeling a lot of internal conflict. Something huge was happening between us and inside of me, and it basically meant that just about everything I had learned about working with horses was false. Before working with Shai in this different approach, I had learned the same way anyone else would—through books, clinics, mentoring under others, and my own experience. Unfortunately, I had discovered something really disturbing. My experiences, though the most important of all my learning methods with horses, were tainted by the perspective I had had at those times. I was working with horses using commonly accepted methods that resulted in an entirely different truth about what horses are and how they behave. Something as basic as haltering your horse to spend time with him can change everything about the way he presents himself to you.

Every day, I was being humbled by this magnificent stallion. He showed me very quickly that I knew far less than I thought I did, and yet many considered me an authority on horses. It was bewildering to realize just how much we humans had wrong about these incredible animals—about all animals. His intelligence level was like nothing I had experienced with another horse. I felt stupid in his presence more than once, when it would be obvious through his frustration that I didn't understand something he was trying to convey. The things I asked of him he learned so quickly and without the need for repetition most of the time. In all my days as a horse trainer, it was heavily ingrained to always "end on a positive note," as in don't stop until the animal you're working with is showing some sort of understanding of what you want. That's not how we did it, though. If Shai didn't want to do what I asked, I had to walk away and try again later or even the next day. More often than not, by allowing him that freedom and showing him respect for his opinion, he did what I asked the next time on the very first try. I could not make sense of it. It made perfect sense in what I knew about building a relationship with another human, but he was a horse! The illusion that I called my reality was beginning to crack.

Other than our actual lessons, we did a lot of wild playing. Basically, that would involve Shai chasing me and flying through the air with his hooves flailing, rearing up right in front of me, and all sorts of scary and dangerous antics such as that. Those were my favorite times, but I had nothing to go on regarding why I wasn't getting hurt or how I was able to get him to calm down without killing me. After a few close calls, and after witnessing Shai calm himself in response to me in ways that I simply couldn't understand, I began to get really worried that I was going to get seriously hurt, and I didn't want to ruin the beauty of what we were doing for everyone else by being an idiot. I had people really interested in what was happening, and they were asking great questions and wanting to do things differently for the good of their own horses. I didn't want to screw that up by allowing my ego to get me kicked in the head just so I could show off my big powerful stallion.

Shai had humbled me down enough, and I had seen too much that I couldn't explain. I decided it was time to stop being an asshole and join the online forum for Nevzorov Haute Ecole—the first step to joining the NHE School. It was there that I gained more understanding about what was happening. I also got a ton of support as well as structure and a safe place to report on my experiences among people who already understood why I was choosing to be with horses this way. I found no dogma or rigidity, only intelligent people who were unwilling to go backward on the truth revealed from working with horses this way. If you could prove your perspective through your own being and experiences with clear logic and respect, they seemed always willing to listen. I shut down Shai's Facebook page, and I apologized to our followers. Our relationship had become too special to exploit, and I no longer felt comfortable making it a public affair.

Once I was on the forum, I had access to a lot more information that helped explain some of what I had been experiencing. It also helped me recognize a "no" even better than I had been, and that's when the film reel began in my mind. I sat down one afternoon, and I swear I even heard the flutter of an old projector as it changed slides, slowly at first, and then click, click, click, click-click-click-clickclickclickclick. I felt empty inside. In just a few minutes, my brain replayed thousands of scenes from my past where a horse had told me no, and I did not listen. It was worse than that, though. Not ready to fully realize the other part of that lesson just yet, I got a glimpse of a thought. I didn't listen too well to the people in my life either. Pat Parelli is widely quoted for saying, "If your horse says no, you either asked the wrong question, or asked the question wrong." I used to believe that. Then I realized that I had started changing my questions and my asking to get what I wanted without any regard for the personal needs of the horse, or the person, I was asking.

It was time to get really honest with myself. I no longer wanted to ride. Having specialized in starting colts for years and having trained many, many horses, it was so clearly obvious to me that horses did not desire us on their backs. I had not met a horse who without any previous training or conditioning had walked up and invited me to hop on top of them like a predator. I knew it could be done in a way that didn't harm the horse and with the horse's true consent, as Alexander Nevzo-rov had already proved, but did I really need to reinvent the wheel? Many of his students had already achieved this as well. I knew the truth, and my ego no longer needed the glory. The NHE School required all students to give up riding before they could be accepted, for good reason. If you still needed to ride, you missed the point, which was the relationship with your horse. Riding added absolutely nothing to the relationship, and if you didn't understand or believe that, then you hadn't actually achieved the relationship. I was ready.

FOURTEEN

-Wide Awake-

*"People think a soul mate is your perfect fit, and that's what
everyone wants. But a true soul mate is a mirror, the person who
shows you everything that is holding you back, the person who
brings you to your own attention so you can change your life."*
~ Elizabeth Gilbert

{I was so torn about what to do with you. I had an obligation to train you because you were not my horse, and I had already promised to do so. I no longer wanted to be on your back or to force you to learn things I could feel you were not interested in learning. However, if not me, then someone else would train you, and they might not be as kind to you. I was so torn.

I heard all the voices around me. All the reasons why it was OK to ride. All the projections and opinions of humans telling me how you felt about us being up there. I listened to those I respected most, and then I looked in your eyes and saw a different truth. I heard their reasoning, and I could understand it, but something just kept tugging. Something told me to ask you, and only you.

I took you home where we could be alone. I talked to you as if you were an old friend. I explained to you that I could hear your resistance to being trained but that I was not the one in charge of your care, and I had promised to do the work. At that point, I really didn't know if riding was OK or not, but it no longer felt like something good inside. I decided to ask you, point blank, if it was OK for me to be on your back.

I climbed on board, and I placed my hands palm down across your withers, gently and lovingly. I asked, "Cisco, is it OK with you for me to be on your back and training you?" I felt your body stiffen. Then you let out a deep sigh and dropped your head, and your body relaxed. I had your permission. My eyes welled up, I slid off your back, and I never climbed on top of another horse again.}

++++++++++++++

One problem with deciding to no longer ride horses when you are a horse professional is that you have to break a lot of promises. I tried to fulfill my remaining training obligations, and the strangest thing happened. I started getting bucked off for the first time in years. Horses I had been riding for months threw me at the first sign that all my fight had left me. This happened four times in less than a month. I had to be honest with the people I had made promises to that I simply could no longer train horses. Then I had to say I could no longer sell horses for them. It was the most humbling experience of my life…to have the skills to train horses and tell people who thought I must have lost my mind that I couldn't do it any longer. I had to look into the eyes of horses I cared about and say, "I'm sorry. I already have too many to take care of." That was really hard. They knew what I understood, and I could not offer them the same life that I was now choosing to provide for the horses in my own pasture. I had 12 horses when Shai came into my life as number 13. Most were intended for business use or to be resold at some point, and when I shifted, I promised each one of them that I would keep them safe for the rest of their lives. It was a lofty promise to make given how my career, which had sustained them thus far, was pretty much over.

My primary source of income at the time was my hoof care business. I was still a full-time barefoot trimmer, but even that no longer felt good to me. As months went by, and we treated all of the horses in our pasture with the same understanding and respect I had learned to bring to Shai, everything changed. Our herd grew healthier and stronger than we had ever seen them. The dynamics within the group changed, and very quickly we realized that our understanding of hierarchy and natural behavior within a herd of horses was based on something far different than what we had now created at home. We had restored balance and harmony to their lives, which changed their so-called natural behavior that is mostly based on survival. When survival is no longer a concern—and it is for many a domestic horse—then the natural state is one far more peaceful than what we were used to observing. As our horses healed mentally, emotionally, and physically from the demands of domestication, training, and riding, they became a harmonious group. No more lead horse displaying aggressive forms of dominance. No more fighting. They now found us interesting, and they began wanting to share space with us in the most awesome and peaceful of ways. Their eyes began changing. That's how I really knew something was different. One by one, the glossy stares disappeared, the veil of old hurts lifted, and I began to meet my own horses, the same way I met Shai, for the very first time. Some of it seemed vaguely familiar—that's when I thought back to the time we had just our two mares and had quit riding for over a year. We experienced similar circumstances with them during that time but had attributed it to their new hoof care, and unfortunately, we lacked the knowledge and awareness to recognize what was really happening. They had been healing.

It was a truly difficult time in my life. What Shai had revealed to me about the true nature of horses flew right in the face of what the world at large currently accepted about them. Every day, we experienced it a bit more deeply and were shaken a bit more and forced to question a lot more about life than horses. I would discuss what was happening with my hoof care clients, and it was obviously challenging for them. The hard part, though, was seeing them get tears in their eyes and tell me they could hear the truth in my words but that they could never give up riding—that it was their only escape, their only joy in life. Others got downright angry. Keep in mind that I wasn't telling anyone to stop riding their horses; I was simply sharing what I had experienced and that I had decided to stop myself. I had one client pretty much yelling at me that she didn't go to a job she hated so she could pay for her fancy barn and the four horses that lived there just to not ride them. They were going to earn their keep. I heard that last statement quite often, actually. My decision to stop riding held up a mirror to everyone, and it reflected their own uncomfortable, guilt-laden, and very attached relationships to their own horses.

What I couldn't explain well to people was that our horses were earning their keep, so to say, far better than they ever did when we were on their backs. I was learning from them and experiencing them in ways that brought profoundly positive changes to my life, despite how difficult those changes sometimes were to navigate. Some of it shook up my personal life and broke me open in painful and confronting ways, but it was making me a better person. The important part was that, because of the relationships I had been developing with the horses on these new terms, riding didn't even seem tempting any longer. I missed the way it felt to control and be powerful over the horses, but that wasn't something I wanted to miss, and my life had more peace and harmony where the horses were concerned than ever before. Peace and harmony were beginning to take the place of anger and control in my life. That is what I wanted.

My training career was over. My hoof care career didn't feel good to me anymore, especially now that I was able to trim all of my own horses free out in the pasture without even a halter. To go out in public and have to deal with other horses in all sorts of various situations, including many with a lot of pain, was horrible by comparison. Even when I began trimming many of my clients' horses the same way as mine, it still wasn't the same. Oftentimes either the horse was checked out and off in some faraway place in his mind or, like the last few I was riding, the horse would realize I had no fight left and give me a hard time after many months of never being trouble to trim. Before, they knew they couldn't get away with it, because I would use my training experience to get them back under control. Now, I would only resort to relationship building, and that did not go hand-in-hand with keeping a timely schedule. Turns out that much like the riding, horses don't exactly appreciate having their hooves trimmed just because someone shows up and says that's what time it is. I didn't know how to make my new understanding work with being a professional in the horse world any longer.

Creating a sanctuary and education center seemed like the only answer I could come up with that felt right inside. I began pursuing that while training an apprentice to take over my hoof care business so I could do that work less and less and put all of my focus into creating a sanctuary for the horses and educating the public with what they were teaching us. I was having a heck of a time getting the support I needed for such a drastic change in direction from my circles in Texas, especially since I was well-known for the work I did that no longer resembled the work I wanted to pursue. Not riding was putting me at odds with a lot of people, no matter how well I presented my reasons why. I was beginning to get a little desperate when I befriended another student in NHE who shared a similar vision and desire. She was in a different part of the country, and I arranged a visit to discuss our ideas of a sanctuary a bit further. I had no idea that my world as I knew it was about to implode.

There was an instant connection when we met at the airport. I knew her. I still can't explain exactly what that means, but something inside me recognized her. It was so obvious that, when I turned back to look at Brandy with a bewildered stare, she indicated that she had seen what just transpired between this stranger and me as well. For as much as I had learned thus far in life, I was being thrown a curve ball that would wake me up and expose every bit of darkness that still lived inside of me. Call it love at first sight—maybe it was lust at first sight—I don't know. What I do know is that I had met a soul mate, maybe even my twin flame, and I was just stupid enough to think that meant we belonged together no matter what the cost. I spent the next five months honestly and openly exploring my feelings for this new woman, and eventually Brandy and I lovingly and respectfully uncoupled, only in part because I had completely and hopelessly fallen for someone else.

My time during this period was divided pretty evenly between visiting her 2,000 miles away, further developing my relationship with Shai, and maintaining my hoof care clients in Texas. It was an absolute roller coaster of emotions, terrible decisions, and life experience that I wouldn't trade for anything. My only regret is that during that time my blind selfishness and my inability to listen often resulted in hurting people I cared for deeply. They don't call it being "madly in love" for no reason. I was unraveling, and there was little I could do to stop it. I had given up all of my control over horses, and now the controlling behavior I had fine-tuned through training horses was being used on the people I cared about most, and in ways I couldn't even see at the time.

I want to tell you what a "horse whisperer" really is. I was labeled with such a term on occasion in my training days, and it's not a term I think of in a positive light any longer. To me, it simply means that you've become so good at manipulating and using subtle forms of psychological control that few can see that you're actually still using massive forms of coercion to get the result you want. I didn't come by this skill on purpose. I mean I don't believe that anyone actually wants that kind of power over another, unless they have a psychological condition. However, because training horses is a celebrated way of developing such a skill, it shouldn't surprise anyone to learn that it does leak into your human relationships as well, especially if it was highly present amongst the adults in your childhood. As it turns out, I had become a highly manipulative individual without even knowing it, and I had been developing my craft through horsemanship for more than half my life.

When you have such a dark talent, and you use it, it really does not matter how pure your intentions may be. It really does not matter how much actual love you may have for a person, or a horse. You will never achieve the desired goal of your heart if your method for getting there is out of alignment with love. I sometimes wish Shai had taught me his most valuable lesson to date before I ever met the woman that mirrored and exposed my darkness, but without the ensuing pain, my heart wouldn't have been broken open enough to receive his gift, or hers.

For many reasons, many due to my lack of integrity during this misguided romance, my new love affair ended as abruptly as it started. The waves of repercussions flowed through my life for months, in areas I never expected them to reach. To feel such shame and heartbreak combined with everything else I was being faced with through my new understanding of horses was daunting. The worst part was that I really did love the people involved, and I had failed so much to show them that I was then shunned in the worst of ways. The situation forced me to be on my own for a while, for the very first time. That is when I got a really good picture of just how far some of my behavior had gotten away from who I really was. For a few months, Shai was my only respite. He was the one relationship I had managed to do right, and one afternoon, he showed me exactly why.

I was in a terrible mood that day. My heart was aching, I was seething with guilt and remorse toward so many people, and I was terrified because the future I had been planning was now out of the question, and I did not have a backup plan. It wasn't a good day to give a lesson to Shai, but it turned out that it was a perfect day for him to assume the role of teacher.

My first mistake was that I entered his pen with an agenda. That's a rule breaker when you're working with horses this way. I was also clearly agitated and hurting, but not in a vulnerable or open way. I was exploding with emotion on the inside, and Shai is not someone you can hide anything from. Things got wild pretty quickly. I wanted the big stuff. I wanted him to rear up tall on his hind legs and pose for me. I wanted to regain some sort of control of my life, and yet I walked in his pen forgetting that it was one place that I clearly had none at all. He was flying all over the place, becoming agitated at me, and beginning to show some aggression, but I wasn't willing to leave that day, so fear began to sink in. Who cares? I had already screwed up my life again, so what if his hoof lands on the top of my head? I snapped out of that thinking pretty quickly. What he and I had achieved already meant far too much to me to give up on now. I took several breaths, trying to regain my composure. Fear was one emotion that Shai was not very tolerant of. He almost seemed to take it personally, as if it were the highest offense to be afraid of someone you claimed to love. Fear and love don't really go hand in hand.

I couldn't get him to calm down. I was a mess. I started crying. I looked down at the ground as my tears landed drop by drop onto the sand under my feet. In that moment, the very second I surrendered and became authentically vulnerable, even weak as I had previously believed, Shai stopped jumping around. His front hooves landed back on the ground with a soft thud. He yawned. He gracefully and gently walked right up to me, and he put his forehead against my chest. It was as if he said, "There now. That's who you are. Feel it." I dropped down to my knees, and as my forehead rested against his soft muzzle, he held a quiet space for me as I realized that I had never loved anyone unconditionally, at least not in my actions, in my entire life. Until him.

FIFTEEN

-Unconditional-

"Ring the bells that still can ring. Forget your perfect offering. There is a crack in everything. That's how the light gets in."
~ Leonard Cohen

{Time with you before was usually spent completely born of my own desires. Now, I couldn't even stand quietly beside you without tears, sometimes heaves of emotion spilling out. My healing was beginning. My pain was finally softening. There were always moments in the past when I felt you were there for me in my vulnerability, but as magical as they seemed, nothing compared to what you were able to offer now.

I had a particularly difficult day. I no longer wanted to impose my hurts upon you, even if it only looked like stroking your strong, soft neck in order to feel better. Even that was now something I considered less than you deserved, unless you offered it of your own free will. So, when I entered the pasture that evening, emotion brimming and about to spill over, I sought out a quiet place far away from the herd, to deal with my hurts alone.

Lost in my sorrow, head down, sitting on the ground under a dark sky, I felt a presence emerge around me. I felt you, and I soaked in the knowing that you were there even though we had not touched, and I had not heard you approach. I was grateful that you had chosen to come stand beside me, and I did not feel alone. When I raised my eyes to see who had come, it was not one. It was three. Spaced equally apart, forming a circle around me. Travis, Cogar, and Velvet. My strong team of support, my friends, my loves.

I knew in that moment that we were truly creating something special together. Your strength and the fullness of your own healing sharing space with my broken messiness filled me with hope. I did not have to go to you and use you to feel better. You chose to share space with me. You chose to stand together in harmony, as a team, and you now could because your own pain had so diminished, and I was finally willing to fully expose myself, even in the dark. You chose to show me that there was nothing about my messiness you needed to walk away from. By allowing you to be fully who you are, you could stand beside me and remind me of who I am underneath the pain. That was the gift of loving you unconditionally.}

+++++++++++++

We all have a darkness to us that balances out the light. The most valuable lesson I have learned to date is to embrace every bit of it, every aspect of who you are, unapologetically. Everyone talks about unconditional love as if they know what it means. I surely did. I am certain that I understood it as a concept, but until that moment with Shai, I was completely blind to just how little I truly exhibited it in my day-to-day life and relationships. I knew what it felt like. I had both loved and been loved unconditionally in many moments, but to be truly loved in that way fully? What was that? It was exactly what I had been practicing with Shai and the other horses over the past several months. It was an allowing—a commitment to love him exactly as he is, with no expectation, no agenda, and no attachment in regard to my own needs and desires. It was total acceptance of what is true in each moment. It was taking responsibility for myself. What it created between him and me was nothing less than the most beautiful relationship I had ever been a part of. It was pure, and it was perfect. Strangely enough, it also produced results far beyond what I was seeking through training, only they were able to be fully realized, they were lasting, and they were authentic.

I had experienced moments of that kind of love in my human relationships for sure. I believe unconditional love exists under the current of basic dysfunction that most relationships are made of. I had glimpsed it and experienced it enough to use it as the main motivation to continue through the suffering of my life, hoping that somehow and someday I would be able to grasp it again, more fully. What I didn't realize is that I had it all along. It lived inside of me. More than that even, I was unconditional love, and I had simply forgotten. I discovered that all my struggles, all of my pain, had come from a lifetime of seeking that love outside of myself, but especially through animals, who had overwhelmingly become a source of instant unconditional love that could be purchased or created at will. I began to look at domestication and keeping pets in a whole new light. It was a light that exposed the truth of our need for domestication in the first place, our refusal to give to ourselves what we seek from others.

All my life, I had been relying on the power of others to move forward with confidence. Whether it was the surface-level confidence I gained from my prowess on the back of a horse, having a beautiful woman fall in love with me, or the constant seeking of a teacher who knew more than I did in any given area, I was always riding high on whatever I could see in another that I refused to see existed in me all along. When I wanted freedom, I could take it from a horse. When I wanted connection, I could manipulate or train someone to give me what connection looked like, but it wouldn't last. Take away the horses, my beautiful partner, excellent teachers, and a myriad of other sources that made me look really good on the surface, and what did I have left? What did I have when it was really just me? Words. I had words, and cogent words at that. For as much as I talked out loud, you should have heard the enormous amount of chatter in my head. I had learned so much about so many aspects of life, and yet, so much of it had not been ingrained in my own. No wonder so many people could not hear the messages of truth I had to share. I was often too much of a walking contradiction for anyone carrying their own pain to be able to take me seriously. Some, though, could sense that what I was beginning to know lived beneath my damaged ego, and they held me up. The horses, however, had something far more powerful to offer.

When I used to ride and train horses, I experienced horses much the same way most of the rest of the world does. Along the way, I discovered a lot of inconsistencies in the information available about horse behavior, care, management, and training. It became an overwhelming process to pick through so many contradictions as I tried to make the best decisions possible for the animals in my care. Being a professional, I interacted with many, many other horse people experiencing the same dilemma. I was determined to find the truth. When I finally reached what is now my truth concerning horses, it was obvious why everyone had a million different answers to avoid it. They might have to change careers, as I did. They might have to re-evaluate their romantic relationships, as I did. They might have to look at every relationship in their life and begin to see how they might not be taking responsibility for their part in anything that wasn't working. Realizing the truth of our relationship to horses would mean a lot of change, especially for an industry that makes billions of dollars a year at the expense of the animal it claims to revere. It was Upton Sinclair who once said, "It is difficult to get a man to understand something when his salary depends on his not understanding it." I found this to be so very true along the way for most people.

The way the world currently treats horses is anything but unconditional. Everyone I know claims to love their horse, but when you really take a good, long look at what that love looks like, is it real? Is putting a piece of metal in someone's mouth to control them love? Is conditioning them to carry you around for your own enjoyment love? Is placing someone in bondage of some kind whenever you want to spend time with them love? I don't think so. I know we can feel love for horses when we spend time with them this way. I also know I felt love for every person I've ever lost in my life due to unloving behavior. If horses weren't kept in stalls or pastures, I can assure you that most of our traditionally accepted actions toward them would send them running for the hills if they had the opportunity.

I once picked up a well-known book on horse training, authored by a close friend of a friend, trying to allow the words in without judgment. I really wanted to understand how someone so loving could not see what I was seeing about horses. In the book, it mentioned that the key to working with and understanding horses was simply to follow the golden rule—to treat them as you would want to be treated. I agreed with that wholeheartedly. In the photo next to this explanation was a photo of the author holding a beautiful stallion. There was a stud chain in place through his halter. I can't speak for anyone else, but if you put a chain around my delicate face to correct me in the event I should do something that makes you uncomfortable, I promise you will be no friend of mine. Let's face it—I wouldn't let you put the chain, much less the halter, on me in the first place. Where was the disconnect?

Throughout my journeys and education, I met many supposed human masters of the horse. Some I had the great pleasure to call friends—from famous trainers to trick riders, professional cowboys to holistic horse care practitioners, nutritionists and feed developers to human therapists using horses to facilitate healing. Each was amazing and inspiring in their own way, and the more I learned, the more my heart broke for them, myself, and the horses we claimed to love. While each of these people used horses to help others and inspire everything from courage to healing and kindness, behind closed doors, not one of them had peace in their own lives when all distractions were gone. Having gotten to know many of them in the privacy of their own personal worlds, their internal struggle was very much the same as mine and the same as all those they wished to help—unless they were using a horse to do the work. Without the horses, they didn't even know who they were. It wasn't their power they were sharing with the world. It wasn't my power I was sharing with the world. It was that of the animals.

From the moment I decided to stop riding on the power of horses, both literally and figuratively, I began to reclaim my own. By power, I mean all I have been gifted with as a human being to create the life of my dreams and be happy. I had been so busy trying to control things, other beings, and situations outside of myself that I never really developed the only skill that mattered—control over my own thoughts, words, and actions. Conscious choices in those three areas, the only areas over which we really do have any control, are what determine our reality in this lifetime. Of that, I'm sure, and I had spent my entire life thus far trying to control everything but myself in order to get what I wanted or needed. I caused a lot of pain along the way, especially to horses, but the one who suffered the most was probably me.

You may notice that there is a lot of information missing from my story, especially the specific scientific proof that helped determine my truth around horses. I left it out for a reason. I gave up trying to convince anyone of anything a while back, and that is definitely not the purpose of sharing my experience now. The science surrounding the harm we cause to horses through riding and training them as well as the way we are taught to keep them at home is alarming to say the least. It's also readily available to anyone who really wants to know, and it's easy enough to find for those looking for it. Throughout the process of my own growth, I've learned something really important about change. Real, lasting change cannot be born from guilt or shame. It only takes place when one wants to embrace it and grow, adding to their human experience, their contribution. Guilt and shame are best friends with self-judgment and self-loathing. If you make changes in your life based on either of them, you've basically changed because you don't accept yourself the way you are. That kind of change will only lead to more shame, even if your actions look different on the surface. I've met a lot of self-righteous people along the way, having been one myself for a very long time, who made changes to their diet or how they related to horses because one way was "right" and one way was "wrong," and let me tell you something about those people—they're still struggling in the exact same ways as the people they determined to be "wrong." Creating polarity is not an avenue to peace—embodying love is. That means loving not just the actions you agree with and the people you agree with, but embracing it all while being a loving example of your own truth. If you enjoy riding and training horses, you should probably keep doing it. The point is to start looking at what is really going on and asking yourself why.

When I fully explored why I was doing what I was doing and what it was doing to the animals I claimed to love, all my desire to ride them disappeared, and it was replaced with something infinitely more fulfilling in my life.

The most difficult part to explain to people who have not met my horses in their new healed state is how very different they are from the horses they used to be and from most horses you are likely to meet. It is something that must be experienced to understand it. To spend time in their presence has turned into the most profound spiritual practice I have found in my life, far more beneficial than when I have tried repeatedly to meditate. For some time, being with the horses in this way was the only positive and healthy way I had found to quiet my mind and listen to my inner knowing. I wanted to share it with everyone.

I began having experimental gatherings at my place to invite people to experience our horses in this new, unconditional way. The feedback was amazing, and each one of the gatherings felt hugely successful, but there was one problem. People with horses, who made up the largest group of people I knew at the time, would come and be really drawn in by it all, but then they would return home and be confronted with their current situation and would be without enough support to make changes in their own horses' lives. That was especially true when they would talk to their friends and family who had horses and did not know anything about what I was trying to share. Most of them wouldn't return to the next gathering. The people without horses in their lives, however, were deeply touched in lasting ways. Not only did they return time and again, they shared what they had experienced with others, and they did it joyfully.

I was seeing people come to my home and experience bits and pieces of what I had promised them, but it wasn't following them home long-term. I realized that I had a huge advantage keeping me strong—I had a very solid and unconditional support system at home in the form of my loving partner, even if the nature of our relationship had since changed to a more platonic state. And because of my history—and let's face it, my personality—no one was going to look at me and tell me what I was doing with my horses didn't make sense, at least not to my face. Most of my guests would have a wonderful experience, which was communicated to me through the evaluation forms I would have them fill out, but then they would return home to a world full of horse people pressuring them to continue doing what was normal and superficially fulfilling. I was beginning to doubt my abilities to make my dream happen in Texas. I needed support, and I needed space to continue my own work with this new paradigm. I decided to contact Stormy May, the creator of the film that changed my life—*The Path of the Horse*.

SIXTEEN

-Good Chocolate-

"Out of all-inclusive, unconditional compassion comes the healing of all mankind."
~ David R. Hawkins, M.D., Ph.D.

{You surprised me most of all. You were given to me because you were hard to catch, difficult to work with, and you bucked. I knew you bucked. You tried to send me flying twice, but that was when I found that kind of challenge fun. You were the pony of my dreams, and now you are still the most perfect, little, stocky, buckskin horse I have ever laid eyes on. I love your beautiful face, and I'm blown away by the capacity of your soul.

You noticed right away when we began to treat you all differently. Everyone was surprised by how you suddenly became friendly and wanted to be near people. People who knew you before didn't recognize you though you physically looked the same. I noticed how easy it suddenly was to take care of your hooves, how trusting you became when you no longer had to be haltered or controlled in some way.

Each morning I would go out to sit in the pasture, and secretly I always hoped you would be one of the horses to come say hello. One day, everyone else was busy eating or exploring, but you noticed me sitting against the base of the big oak tree. You walked over and rested your muzzle on the top of my head. I was still new to this closeness, this allowing, and the trusting that you would not hurt me in your new state of awareness. You began to move your lips back and forth through my hair, grooming me the way you would one of your equine friends.

You moved your lips to my face. You licked my cheek. I didn't move. I breathed and remained calm, staying present and completely aware in case I needed to let you know I was uncomfortable. You put your lips around my nose. I was beginning to get nervous, but everything I had learned had taught me to trust you, to just stay present. I heard your teeth separate. I asked you out loud to please be careful and not to bite me. For some reason, I completely surrendered. Your teeth opened around my nose, and you just stood there, perfectly still, my delicate feature between your teeth. A few moments passed, and you pulled your face just far enough away to make eye contact with me. I swear you smiled.

I wasn't sure what exactly to make of what had just transpired between us, but I have now since seen similar behavior between you and many of the others in your herd. It's a friendly gesture that I have never seen escalate to anything harmful. It was intimate, sweet, and full of trust. You gave me hope that I could someday share that kind of intimacy with another human, without it ever needing to be more than two souls meeting in a moment of truth.}

++++++++++++++

I met Stormy in November of 2012, in New York, at a film screening for her documentary. We shared a lovely weekend together and became close friends. The next month I flew out to her home in Northern California to meet her family and continue our discussions about creating a sanctuary for horses and humans. It was so comforting to be around other people who not only understood but were willing to continue to question what many others were afraid to even look at. During my next visit, she took me to meet more people who understood the horses this way, who had already left their old lives behind to create sanctuaries for the horses. The energy of this area was so different than back at home. People seemed different here too. Brandy joined me on this visit, and we both fell in love with everything the area had to offer. Within a few short months, we left Texas to create a new life around what the horses had taught us. Just south of the Oregon border, we found a new place to call home.

It wasn't a well-thought-out decision, but we didn't care. I knew I had done everything I could do at that time in Texas, and I needed to remove myself and have the freedom to explore my new truth in peace. I had no idea just how big of a leap we were taking. In May of 2013, we were told about a small piece of property that could support us and our animals in the high desert north of Mt. Shasta. By July, we had purchased that property and sold off pretty much everything we owned at the time that could not fit into our small cargo trailer or the RV we purchased to make the trip that would be our new home. We spent our entire savings to make the journey and to ship the horses as one big group, and I left my business behind for my apprentice to slowly take over in the course of the next year.

So in just a few months' time, I went from having a pretty normal life with two new vehicles in the driveway, a big house, and plenty of income to living completely off the grid in the desert in a tiny travel trailer, with one vehicle between two people sharing a common vision, and thirteen horses, five dogs, three cats, and three pigs to take care of on one income—all done in the name of following a dream and pursuing truth in honor of the horses that changed our lives. I must say, looking back, I might have done things a tad bit differently.

Just before we left Texas, I went on a wilderness quest that included a two-day, two-night solo fast with nothing but a backpack and very basic survival equipment. It was the absolute first time in my life that I had ever spent a day, much less 48 hours, completely and utterly alone with only my thoughts and not a single distraction from them. It was a terrifying and uncomfortable experience, and it also showed me just how far from inner peace I really was when left solely to my own devices. Never did it sink in so much how I had been relying on animals and other people to feel OK in the world. It really brought the truth home about how much I had been avoiding myself all those years, using comfort, control, and horses as a distraction from facing my own inner turmoil. It gave me a brief understanding of what was to come, but I had no way of knowing just how much I was about to completely unravel.

Our new friends went above and beyond to care for our horses until we arrived and could get settled. There was the potential for us to work together, but in only a short time that would fall apart. Out in the desert, far from close friends and family, living in a way I was totally unprepared for, in an environment very new to me in every way, I came undone. With Brandy in a job that kept her away more often than not, I was left alone in the desert to deal with myself and take care of 25 animals I had come to see as my equals. I quickly realized that I did not even know how to take care of myself under these conditions, much less them. It was, and in some ways continues to be, the most difficult challenge of my life. There is nothing easy about facing yourself when you have been running for so very long, and yet, I was tired of running and couldn't imagine making any other choice at that point.

We have made a lot of choices, especially financially, since coming here that have not served us well. When you are far removed from all of the ways you have been supported in the past, it is overwhelming how much you realize you have been addicted to things, benign things, for so long. You also realize just how much you have taken for granted, like always having access to warmth and a flushing toilet. There is no cure for loneliness out here other than to learn to love yourself. There is no cure for mind chatter other than to become a compassionate and nonjudgmental observer of your thoughts. It's been scary and difficult at times, and yet, I am never very far away from a deep feeling of peace and surrender that was not a part of my life before now. It has been a struggle, and the struggle isn't over, but we move forward, day by day, toward the dream of becoming living examples of the unconditional love modeled through our horses and in our care of them. It has forced us to make some very difficult decisions in our personal lives to become as healed and whole as we can be as individuals in order to offer more to one another and the rest of the world.

I'm no longer interested in making a name for myself. Now, I simply want to be an authentic example of what I believe is the answer to all the world's major problems—love. I wish only to seek truth, be love, and have the courage to do those things. I have 30 years of bad habits going against one year of new understanding, so I'm a long way off, but I'm committed to the process, and I have the horses to remind me what it looks like every single day. They have become a powerful example of healing and harmony and just how much can change when you are supported unconditionally, and I have hope that if people could learn to treat one another the way we have learned to treat these horses, there's a chance for a better world—for humans, for horses, for all of us. As long as the world is wrapped up in this business of right and wrong, we will suffer. The nature of who and what we are, underneath all the ego, is unconditional love, where right and wrong simply do not exist, where understanding takes the place of judgment. The closer we get to who we truly are, the less pain and suffering we want to inflict on ourselves or the rest of the world. I believe that is the key—not in changing our actions out of guilt, shame, or some moral obligation, but by allowing our harmful actions to change through our state of being. We must consciously choose to move toward a higher state of being if we want lasting change on this planet. We must have the courage to seek out truth, no matter how uncomfortable it may be, so that we know what to move away from that is no longer serving us. When I act out of love, my choices are in alignment with love. When I act out of fear, even if the action looks the same on the surface, the underlying energy hasn't changed, and I am perpetuating the same problems I want to solve.

I understand the fear. I still feel it myself some days, though it doesn't even compare to what I felt in the past. It is super scary to walk away from anything that feels safe and jump into the unknown, but I didn't come here to feel safe. I came here to live. I came here to know and understand all that it means to be human and to fall in love with who and what I am over and over again. We are amazing beings with massive creative potential, potential that is so very often wasted in activities like dominating horses so we can ride them around for fun. We get sucked into activities like this, and they become addictive because they allow us to avoid facing our pain, to run away from it all. However, it's in the facing of our fears that we become courageous and that we get to experience the real joys and pleasures that this life has to offer us. There is no freedom where there is fear.

I have spent just a little over a year out in the desert with my horses and other animal friends. It has not been easy. There have been times when I have questioned my sanity, when I have wanted out, when I have come down so hard on myself for putting us through so much drastic and difficult change. I have noticed, though, that when I do venture out to be with other people I am kinder than I once was. I am learning to listen, but more importantly, I really want to listen. My inner pain level has been so reduced that I can often share space with someone in a lot of pain and not be negatively affected. I can be a source of comfort for those in need. I am no longer quick to anger. I no longer feel the need to defend myself or argue about much of anything, and that is huge for me, especially in regard to horses. There are so many changes in me that are so obvious to those who knew me before and now that I can no longer question the validity of my reasons for doing this. I am healing, and I am becoming the best version of myself, even if it takes time. I really got to see for myself just how much I had changed recently. A little over a year after my first wildness quest, I was fortunate to take part in another one out in the wilds of Oregon. This one included a three-day, three-night solo fast. Not only was it not difficult this time and not only had I made friends with my mind and thoughts, but if I'm being completely honest—it felt like a freaking vacation compared to my normal day-to-day life at the sanctuary! I am stronger than I have ever been, and even though it is all still very challenging and I still have a tremendous amount of work to do, I believe in myself and in the message I came here to share. I would like to share some of that message now.

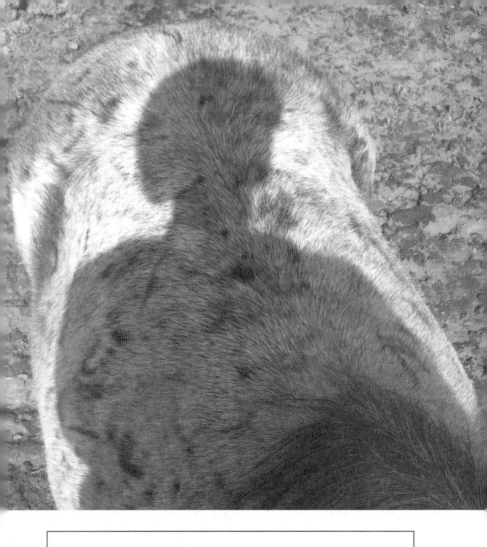

SEVENTEEN

-Power & Responsibility-

"Power over others is weakness disguised as strength."
~ Eckhart Tolle

{Giving up riding, for me, was like an alcoholic choosing to walk away from drinking. Intellectually, even in my heart, I no longer wanted it in my life because I knew it no longer served me, but the craving was still there sometimes. I maintained a glimmer of hope that maybe I had it all wrong, that maybe you really didn't mind me climbing on board for a joy ride. Maybe you loved me enough to let me hurt you.

Every few months, if you were near anything that would give me easy access to your back, I would rush over to stand on it and see how you reacted if I indicated I might climb on. Every single time, even after a year of not being ridden, your eyes would widen, your neck would stiffen, and you would step aside. When you were in training and being ridden, you knew better than to move away, and now that you had found your voice, you were clear about your feelings.

Eventually, I truly sobered up and lost all desire to be on top of you. One day, playfully, I climbed on a rock that was next to where you were standing. I leaned across your back, rubbing your body and kissing your soft fur. You didn't budge. You didn't even blink. You remained completely relaxed and at ease, happily munching your hay because you knew beyond any shadow of a doubt that there was no way I would ever take advantage of you again. You knew I had learned to love you, and you loved me enough to not only tell me no when I needed to hear it, but to trust me when I had earned it. I love you so much, my beautiful, black Velvet, and I will never break that trust.}

+++++++++++++

One of the hardest obstacles for me to overcome in this journey has been listening to the people I admire most in my life when they've been in direct opposition to some of my ideas around these topics concerning horses. I owe some of these very people some major credit for helping me become the person I am today, and yet, at some point, their roles as teachers in certain areas of my life had to be let go, and I had to stand strong in my own truth, just as they taught me to do. One area in particular concerns the horse's role in granting permission to be on their backs.

In my introduction to Chapter 14, you met Cisco, the very last horse I rode. I am certain, beyond any doubt, that he granted me permission to be on his back that day. However, it in no way felt like what he wanted for himself, and I had grown far too aware at that point to disregard such things. How often in our daily lives do we grant permission to others at our own expense? How often do we say yes to things we would really rather not do? As someone who spent most of her life just looking for the yes and not the reason behind it, I feel it is very important to discuss the issue of power and responsibility that I have learned from these horses.

When I was very young, I was placed in very damaging sexual situations by an older, and trusted, family member. Did I resist? No. Was I granting permission? It very likely could have been perceived that way because I went along willingly. Even if asked outright, I may have in my childlike mind granted permission to be involved because I simply did not know better. When a young woman says yes before she is ready, is she really OK with it? When someone who has not learned to set boundaries says yes in a situation that actually creates pain for them, does that make it OK? It's a hard question to answer, but here are my thoughts on such things: If the person asking for something is being authentic in their request with no intention of causing harm, and they are granted permission, then they have met their responsibility in the situation. However, when the person asking permission knows of the harm that could be caused from their request, and they move forward anyway, then there is something to be concerned about. At times, I used to be such a person. I wanted what I wanted, and I placed all the responsibility on the other party to say yes or no regardless of whether or not I could feel something different from them. Sometimes I would do the worst thing I could have done, by pursuing the feeling of yes when the word was no, especially if I could tell someone was only saying no out of fear rather than their true desire, which I could feel in their energy and see in their body language thanks to all my experience as a "horse whisperer." I look back now and think that made me a monster, but I'm learning to judge less and understand a little more and find compassion for myself and others like me.

The truth is, it's a difficult topic to discuss and understand. Many of the people who were telling me it was OK to ride horses didn't know the science showing the harm it caused to the animal. I did. So even though I was granted permission, knowing the harm I was causing made me responsible for making a better choice, one that considered the other party equally, despite what they were willing to allow. This also got me thinking about all the opinions I had heard of those who utilize animal communication in their work with horses. Many animal communicators or their clients had told me their horses enjoyed being ridden. I could not understand that for the longest time. I have thirteen horses in my pasture, and with the exception of Shai, not one of them is OK with the idea of being ridden after two years of total freedom; and I've tested that fully just to be absolutely sure. After spending a lot of time with our horses in a healed state, especially Shai, whom I had taken the time to educate and develop on an intellectual level, it became quite obvious what the answer was when I'd go out and be around other horses living the typical domesticated horse life. They were coming from an entirely different perspective. They generally had no idea what life outside of being ridden and trained looked like, much less that it was an option. They were absolutely in a state of learned helplessness, and if you have ever met a person in such a state, you know exactly what I'm talking about. Let's just assume for the sake of argument that animal communication is possible and that these horses had really granted permission or admitted to enjoying being ridden. If I ask a child to make a decision, such as I was when presented with a harmful sexual encounter, would it be responsible of me to assume that the child knew what was best for them? If I ask something of someone who has been controlled for so long that they don't even know what is best for them, should I take advantage of that? What makes us think that the average horse is able to answer such questions about riding from any sort of mature understanding? Most horses are conditioned beyond any hope of being able to confidently express how they really feel. Basically, they are brainwashed and fully indoctrinated into the cult of domestication.

This isn't an issue of right and wrong but rather an issue of responsibility and using our power in a way that serves ourselves and those we care about. When one has power over another, which is always the case in riding horses, it is of extreme importance that such power comes with great responsibility. I have searched and searched for any reason that would make it OK for me to climb up on a horse's back again and enjoy that sensation, and when I fully consider the horse, there is none. The horse does not benefit from my being atop his back, and I put him at great risk of harm even when it is done with total mastery, which is rare. This is an issue of taking a deep look at the things we do and being willing to question their validity in our moving toward the life and the world we hope to create. Do you want a better world? Are your actions in alignment with creating kindness, love, and understanding? If they aren't, there is no hope for change unless you find the courage to face yourself and do something differently.

I think the event that really influenced my desire to look at domesticated animals differently was when I taught Shai colors for the first time. One of my NHE School lessons was to teach Shai different colors and objects and ask him to select the correct color and/or object requested. It took less than fifteen minutes for him to learn the difference between blue, purple, and red, and he never made one mistake. I taught him in the same way I might have taught a young human child. That experience, combined with the videos and material I had been studying of Alexander Nevzorov's own horses with their Latin lessons, caused me to turn around, go in my bedroom, and debate whether or not I would ever come out again. Many times I peeked out my window to stare at this magnificently intelligent being, trapped in a pen so I could play with him and do with him as I pleased, as tears streamed down my face.

Having underestimated the intelligence level of animals for so long and at such great depth, when I was exposed to the truth of what they are really able to understand, being surrounded by them left me feeling like a slave owner. It's no wonder we keep them stupid. Isn't that exactly how we were able to control members of our own species for so long? One will never be able to understand the intellectual capability of another if they are only willing to weigh it against their own understanding of that individual. If we believe animals to be stupid, and we keep them under our control, they will be stupid unless we create an environment and situation where they can advance. I never did another lesson like that with Shai. It served me better to allow him to just be a horse after I realized what he had the potential to become. It took a lot for me to give up what he and I had created together, but when we moved to our little sanctuary in California, I had him gelded and gave him the opportunity to live with other horses for the very first time and be just like them. It took him a while to stop asking me for lessons, but eventually he settled in and became the most popular guy in the pasture. We still have something special, but it's nothing like we used to have, and I wish everyone knew just what kind of actual commitment it would take to truly maintain such a relationship with a horse, especially a stallion. I doubt very many people would want it if they knew just how equal that horse would become.

When the documentary *Blackfish* came out in 2013, it was hard for me to watch—not because of the abuse featured in the film, but because I spent the entire film shaking my head and muttering, "How is this any different than what we do with horses?" I was absolutely thrilled to see the impact this movie made for killer whales kept in captivity, but I was frustrated that the world at large considers it completely acceptable to commit the exact same crimes against horses. For one, horses are no different biologically than their wild counterparts. Two, horses kill people every single day in response to the pain we inflict upon them. Three, I wish everyone knew the average lifespan of a domesticated horse compared to that of a healthy, wild one, just as the film made clear for orcas. We abuse horses in nearly everything we do with them, and because we have been doing it for so long and people love it so much, few seem to care. Oh, I forgot that billions of dollars are generated from our abuse of horses. Does this mean we should turn all the horses out into the wild? Of course not. It just means we could think about not using them for sport or breeding them to be our play things. Instead, maybe we could create sanctuaries, even in our own backyards, and start learning from them to create a better world and be happier, more whole beings ourselves.

I've had so many people want to discuss what I'm doing with horses and then challenge it by saying something along the lines of, "Oh, I could never stop riding; how would I make a living?" or "Do you have any idea how many people would be out of jobs if everyone quit riding horses?" I just look at them blankly as if they did not hear that I had already been down that road and chose something else, and I hadn't died yet. I may not have a large human family, but I do have 25 animals to care for, and we do whatever we have to do to get by. If that means at the end of this year I have to go back to working in an office until I figure out the next step, then that's what I will do. As Antoine de Saint-Exupéry said in *The Little Prince*, "You become responsible, forever, for what you have tamed." I am taking my responsibility very seriously these days. More importantly, I'm taking the time to learn who I am without horses so that I can discover what it is I truly love to do, for myself. Maybe it will be writing. Maybe it will be something else. I don't know, and I don't care; but what I do care about are those I love, and I'm not willing to harm them any longer so that I can reap financial rewards from it.

EIGHTEEN

-Evolution of Food-

"Nothing will benefit human health and increase the chances for survival of life on Earth as much as the evolution to a vegetarian diet."
~ Albert Einstein

{Your little home is a magic place for me to spend time. I just do not know how to be unhappy in your presence. You are easier for me to spend time with than the horses here because I certainly never rode you or hurt you. I obviously didn't eat you, specifically, because you're here, safe and sound for the rest of your life. You make me smile, and I love rubbing your bellies—bellies that were obviously made for scratching and not for eating, in my opinion.

There was a time when I would stress about food going bad before we had time to eat it, especially when finances became quite limited and we began purchasing mostly organic produce. You changed all that. Now, when food is not going to be used by us humans, I get to lovingly prepare it for you instead. Nothing ever goes to waste. It fills me with so much joy to treat you in this way. You are always so happy to receive anything yummy I bring you, and to you, it's all yummy.

Your affinity for beer and wine makes me laugh, but I don't know why it would surprise me. What is beer if not liquid grain? All three of you are some of the most charming beings I have had the pleasure of spending time with, and our lives here would not be the same without you. Starting my days with your amazing range of snorts, oinks, and squeals is something to be grateful for. Thank you, Hercules, Francis, and Samson, for showing me who you are and spending time with me as I heal myself from deep, old wounds. I so enjoy your company, and I am so glad you helped teach me the value of friends over food.}

+++++++++++++

I spent my first thirty years in Texas, where I grew up on a diet that mainly consisted of beef, pork, chicken, cheese, and bread in some combination for most meals. Fast food was a part of my regular menu, and I was an adult before I ever even tasted many vegetables outside of a can. I took a college course that required me to witness the entire slaughter process from live pig to food on the plate, and I happily went out for burgers and ribs afterward with friends. In my late teens, when I became very overweight for a while, my boyfriend and I watched the movie "Supersize Me" and then thought it would be funny to go get the greasiest, nastiest meal possible from a fast food place nearby to celebrate our new education. Needless to say, I have struggled with food addiction, poor nutrition, and weight all of my life. I never imagined I could or would ever have the desire to become a vegetarian, much less eventually move to an entirely plant-based diet, giving up my long-time love affair with cheese.

When Shai entered my life, I wanted to do absolutely every-thing I could to succeed in having a wonderful relationship with him. I had read that horses could smell whether or not I was a meat eater, which might indicate to them I was a predator and make it harder to establish trust. Whether that is true or not is irrelevant, but it did get me thinking that maybe it didn't make so much sense for me to be eating animals and also trying to make my life about forming relationships with them. Contrary to many others at the time, I was for horse slaughter simply because I didn't see the difference between eating horses and eating cows. I found every meat eater who was violently opposed to horse slaughter to be a massive hypocrite. My political science profes-sor in college would be happy to read that, seeing as how back then I argued with him at length about the differences between horses and cows and how it was inherently wrong to eat horses but OK to eat cows because they weren't as intelligent. He was probably a vegetarian, now that I think about it. I might as well have been from a different planet at the time, but I still managed to get an A in that class.

Anyway, I was not about to make such a massive life change based on the balance between good and evil. I needed more information. I began doing research and watching films like *Earthlings* and *Forks Over Knives*. I needed the science behind why it might be a good idea to change my diet. I needed the bigger picture. I had been eating meat—and enjoying it—for a very long time, so damned if I was going to stop all of a sudden because someone said it was wrong. It didn't take much work at all to convince me. The proof I needed was easily found anywhere the information wasn't backed by a corporate agenda, and the implications of continuing to eat animal products actually scared me. I felt so ignorant and misinformed, and I cannot believe that people would still choose to eat meat and dairy just based on taste if they knew the truth of all the harm being caused by one simple choice—what we eat. I cannot stress enough how important it is to have the courage to learn the facts about the choices we make so that we can see what is no longer serving us.

I wanted to be smart about changing my diet. I cut out red meat first, and that was actually the hardest for me. I loved bacon most of all, so I did what anyone might do who was serious about giving it up—I adopted two pigs to love and care for as friends instead of food. Hercules and Francis came from an animal rescue in Missouri, and I loved them immediately. I dare say that had I met pigs in this way before horses I might not have such a story to share today! I adored those pigs and enjoyed spending time with them as much as the horses. Plus, when I applied my new understanding of horses with them, it worked the exact same way and led me to further understand that it didn't matter the species—when met with understanding and unconditional love, the potential for connection and relationship was pretty much limitless. Also, the intelligence level of animals is, again, astounding. After about a month of playing with and loving on piggies, I walked in the house one morning to find my apprentice cooking bacon on the stove. As soon as the smell hit me, I was overwhelmed with a wave of nausea. I was completely flabbergasted. I had LOVED the taste of bacon, but my shift in thinking had completely changed that, right down to my very senses. I was cured—from pork at least.

I continued my learning and phased meat out of my diet. My health improved dramatically in so many ways. It took me a long time to give it up completely. Cheeseburgers especially were a comfort food for me. In times of high stress and anxiety, I would still occasionally eat one and then seriously regret it, because my body was so over meat by then. Thankfully, I've found many delicious vegan alternatives at this point. Dairy was much harder and is still a struggle at times, especially when we go out to eat. It got a lot easier when I got my hands on *The China Study* by Dr. T. Colin Campbell. His brilliant work on the correlation between eating animal products and cancer along with many other life-threatening issues was mind-blowing. Casein was no longer my friend, and just like the bacon, I began to see it much differently when I had the support of good information to counteract my old habits and addictions. The best and most convincing film for me, though, was *Cowspiracy: The Sustainability Secret.* Understanding how my diet choices were affecting the health of the planet was a real wake-up call, and I encourage anyone to watch that film if they do nothing else. I might be biased, because they do bring in the wild horse aspect as well.

I still don't understand why people can be so opposed to switching to a plant-based diet. The proof is out there in waves, unsupported by a capital agenda, and steeped in truth. It is the key to solving most health problems. Eating animal products is the single most destructive force and yet the most solvable issue concerning environmental sustainability and climate change. It is kind and compassionate to the animals, animals we mostly created to be able to eat through domestication. It simply makes sense. We could end world hunger so quickly if we were growing plants on the land that we devastate to raise cattle. We could end the healthcare crisis in America. Don't like GMOs? We probably wouldn't have them if we hadn't needed a way to feed all the animals and help them grow fast to meet the demands of the fast food industry that is killing people every day through the consumption of its poison. On the horse front, many of the people who advocate for wild horses and are angry about their being removed from their natural lands are actually helping to create the problem in the first place by eating meat. The horses are primarily being removed to make room for cattle and sheep to be raised for food. The information surrounding the major problems that could be solved by humanity's embracing a plant-based diet is enough to fill at least 100 books in and of itself, and if you doubt me on that, please be brave enough to do the research.

The biggest fear always seems to be around money or loss of jobs. I wish people would realize that when one thing goes away, something new emerges. Just because it won't look like what you're used to doesn't mean there won't be a solution available. If we weren't pouring valuable time and resources into destroying ourselves and the planet out of greed and a desire for comfort, we might be able to spend our time and talents more wisely by coming up with solutions. People have asked me, "If we didn't ride horses, what would we have done for transportation back when that is how we got around, and how would we have worked the fields?" My answer to that is that it doesn't matter what we did back then—we need to look at what is happening right now. But quite frankly, if we had spent less time using horses that way, maybe we could have used our talents to develop technology a little quicker. When we take the time to question what we are doing and why we are doing it, it is amazing how quickly things can change. Our creative abilities are limitless. We simply have to believe in the possibility of what we want to create and then take steps toward it.

Another concern I often hear with giving up animal products is from people who say they suffered health issues when they tried to switch to a plant-based diet. All I can say to that is, just like anything else, you have to be fully committed to the change in order for it to work and be lasting. If you still want to eat meat, you're not ready to give it up. I have had several people, women especially, tell me they tried to ditch meat but became too weak to do their physically demanding jobs. I was trimming an average of 15 horses per day on a vegetarian diet and never felt stronger. Human beings are not designed to thrive on meat over plant-based foods, and contrary to popular belief, getting enough protein from plants is extremely easy. Many of the health problems experienced when trying to change diets come from the eating of animal products in the first place, and it takes time to heal. Most of what we know about nutrition is funded by an industry that wants you to eat meat and dairy, so what do you think the chances are of it being factual? If the plants you are eating aren't working for you, there is probably more to learn and do differently. I can promise one thing, though—if you try to switch to a plant-based diet out of guilt or out of the desire to "do the right thing," chances are you're setting yourself up for failure. If you really want it, you'll find a way, and it will serve you. You can take your time. It's more important to do what feels right in each moment for you than to make some massive change out of obligation and then beat yourself up if you don't do it perfectly. If you want to eat meat, do it, but please ask yourself why and be willing to investigate the validity of those answers. Again, it's not an issue of right or wrong; it's an issue of sustainability and the avoidance of facing the truth behind how our current systems work and why they are failing us.

As I've mentioned before, when you look at issues in a right-versus-wrong stance, you'll run into a lot of problems around creating viable long-term solutions. When one focuses on elevating the state of their own being toward loving kindness and allowing their choices to flow from that place, it is impossible not to affect change. When you truly heal and transform yourself, you will affect all those around you, at whatever level they are ready to be affected. When you point fingers and place blame, you just piss people off. I know. I've pissed off a lot of people in my relatively short life.

NINETEEN

-Equine-Assisted Psychosis-

"Yes, I'm a dreamer and grandiose at times, but you know something? To the core of my soul, I truly believe the powerful combination of horse and human is an avenue to awareness."
~ Wyatt Webb

{I knew how far we had come when I no longer felt the need to use words or gestures around you. We had developed a language that was all our own, and it had nothing to do with horses or humans. We were simply two different physical expressions of the same larger thing, and I could feel you, and you could feel me. We were the same. And we were different. And that made it wonderful and exciting and interesting.

I once made the mistake of taking a call before I came in to play with you. As I walked around your space, mostly ignoring you while I chatted on the phone, you suddenly came up behind me and pulled the hood of my shirt over my head. I started laughing like crazy because you never ceased to amaze me with your humor and personality. The person on the other end of the phone probably thought I was crazy. I didn't care.

You must have remembered my reaction that day because I still can't wear a hooded shirt or coat around you without your attempting to pull it over my head. I've never actually heard you laugh, but I swear I know what your laughter feels like. You're a funny boy, Shai, and I don't know how to thank you for changing so much in my life. The least I can do is to keep you safe and well for the remainder of yours.}

+++++++++++++

Years ago, when I was sitting in my little office trying to figure out how best to reenter the horse world as a professional, I received something in the mail about a certification program for equine-facilitated therapists and their equine specialists. I knew immediately that is what I wanted to do—to aid skilled and effective therapists with my knowledge and understanding of horses. I could not afford the training, so I took the card I received in the mail and placed it on my vision board, hoping it would move me toward a future of helping people through horses. I trained in hoof care instead, and that eventually led me to trimming for clients who were professionals in this emerging field of equine-assisted psychotherapy.

I tried many times to work with or learn from anyone in this field who came into my space. Many opportunities came up, and something would always happen to keep us from coming together. One of the leaders in this field, who happened to be friends with close connections of the ranch I had been with in Texas, came in from out of state to stay at the ranch and do demonstrations on two different occasions. Both times I was somehow unavailable and unable to meet her or compare notes.

As my own journey with horses progressed, I began to question a lot of what I had learned about the current model of equine-assisted therapy, especially where it concerned the well-being of the horses involved. Having trimmed a handful of horses involved in this type of work, I had an up-close comparison between them and my own horses at home, who were healing and becoming far different creatures than I used to know. Then it finally dawned on me. The entire current model of equine therapy is based on a misunderstanding of horses. The whole industry has based its interactions with horses around what is traditionally accepted about horses and not on what I have spoken of throughout this story. That is a huge problem for people who utilize this kind of therapy for healing, and it is also unfair to the horses in many cases.

I believe that healing cannot occur at the expense of another being. What we have discovered through our own horses, however, is that healing can be facilitated and accelerated by sharing space with them, so long as they are not imposed upon in any way. I can pretty much assure you that most horses used in equine-facilitated therapy are paying dearly for any benefits being derived from their use as therapy horses. Even the ones who are not ridden are usually controlled with ropes, halters, a small enclosed area, mental conditioning, or are in some state of learned helplessness. Many of them are also experiencing physical pain because of the lack of understanding around the world concerning what horses biologically need to be healthy. They are a broken mirror reflecting back an image that cannot lead to actual transformation. Real transformation begins with unconditional love, which is something most horses never receive from the humans who care for them.

What if horses could reflect from a whole and healed place? What if they were safe to be around without ropes or controlling safety precautions because, in their healed state, they exuded peace and harmony and an awareness of their surroundings? What if the most valuable thing horses had to offer us was a supportive space to practice a different state of being? What if by healing horses and loving them in an unconditional way, we could provide a model for healing ourselves and the rest of humanity? I know it sounds lofty, but the parallels between what we have seen with our horses and what I believe is possible between humans are huge. The most important of these is the concept of "the horse is never wrong," which I learned many years ago from Mark Rashid and was implemented further by Alexander Nevzorov. If we applied that same rationale to our fellow humans, imagine the potential. Imagine meeting people where they are, with understanding and compassion for their unique and individual perspective of the world, instead of making them out to be wrong. Imagine if we all reached for understanding instead of placing blame, and we worked with that instead of fighting.

The horses in our backyards have far more value to humanity as a safe way to practice this kind of awareness than they ever would by carrying us around like fools. It is so much easier to be vulnerable in front of a horse than it is to be in front of another human who is most likely carrying a lot of their own pain. It works best with a healed horse in a model of unconditional care, however, because it's the healing presence and the peace and calm around that environment that allows the learning to take place effectively. Loving and caring for horses this way becomes the practice to help facilitate our own healing so that we can then go out in the world and be that healing presence offered to the rest of the world. We don't turn the horses back out into the wild; we care for them and spend time with them in a way that is mutually beneficial; and as humans heal, we slowly release the need to possess the horses in the first place. Am I a dreamer? Sure. And if you haven't noticed, I'm hell bent on following my dreams.

After I moved to California, I was asked to speak to a group of counselors at an equine therapy facility back in Texas. I spent the afternoon speaking of my ideas and experiences to a very engaged group of intelligent women. They loved what I had to say, and they wanted to move forward to change how the horses were cared for and interacted with at the center. I was so thrilled. This was everything I had ever hoped to be able to do through the work I had done so far. We ran into problems quickly, however. So many changes would need to be made to heal the horses there that it was overwhelming for the people in charge. My putting the horses' needs over their use in therapy, and more importantly the income they produced, was too threatening to the people making the decisions. After being told by the manager that they wished to contract with me to implement changes, I returned to California and never heard directly from them again. They wouldn't return my calls, and I was basically ignored by the person in charge of decision making, though I heard bits and pieces from others involved. It was just too much information for people to digest without experiencing it for themselves. It was then that I realized that the only way I was ever going to show people the value of what I had learned was to do it myself, with the horses whose lives I had already changed.

I put my focus back into my own work on myself because it has become very clear to me at this point that, even when I speak with great cogency, if I'm not fully walking my talk, no one will be able to hear me, and all of this will have been for nothing. I'm still in the process and nowhere near ready to help anyone else directly, but now I have a pretty good idea of what needs to be done.

Changing the model of equine-assisted therapy is only one of my goals where psychology is concerned. What I want most is to shed light on the harm that is caused to us when we use horses the way that is traditionally accepted in training, riding, competition, and sport. I am especially concerned when this involves children and teaching them to control horses in such a way. In my experience, the most common thing I've noticed, both with myself and with others who are deeply involved with using horses in these ways, is a disconnection that shuts down the ability to connect and truly feel the energy of others. In order to work with and ride horses the way we commonly do, we have to take control of them, and we very often cause them pain. To do this and enjoy it, we cut ourselves off from feeling their experience, and we disconnect from empathy, which can also have an effect on our relationships outside of horses. It did for me at least.

When I began to approach horses differently and open back up that energetic exchange in order to connect with them, it became impossible for me to be around a horse who was in a great amount of pain without feeling it myself. I had to learn how to tune it out when needed. This was necessary for me to be able to continue doing my job in hoof care since many of the horses I worked on were in pain. Going to a horse show or competition was out of the question. For me, seeing horses ridden for sport, especially when metal and a large amount of control devices is involved, is like watching someone physically abuse their child. It doesn't feel any different to me. I do not judge the abuser, because I fully understand where they are coming from, but it still isn't something that is easy or fun for me to look at. The pain of the horse fully registers with me, and there is very little I can do about it in those moments. We celebrate our abuse of horses, especially in the show ring.

I cannot even describe how much opening up to horses through consciously being present with them has opened me in other areas. I feel energy and emotion from other people that never registered on my radar before. It has helped me tremendously in being able to make helpful choices surrounding those I care about. It has also made me very aware of others' needs even if they lack the ability to communicate those needs effectively. Sometimes it is overwhelming, and I know it is going to take time to get used to and use effectively, but wow. What a gift. The beauty of it is that every single one of us is capable of connecting and feeling at that level and beyond. This ability to be with and feel others can transform even the most difficult relationships, and I've seen it transform how I react to people in pain who may be acting out violently. A year ago I would most likely have fought back, whereas now I can openly receive and just give space more often than not. It's had a tremendous effect on my relationships with people I wouldn't normally get along with, and I'm not nearly as reactive as I once was.

Currently, my great joy in life is working with a group of at-risk teen girls at a farm sanctuary where I volunteer. They inspire me with every visit and motivate me to create a place where programs like theirs can come and where they can learn the value of unconditional love, boundary setting, and respect by spending time with healed horses. Many of them have similar backgrounds to my own, and it feels so amazing to be able to hear and understand what they are going through. I am now grateful for all my struggles because I am finally able to fully realize their value in bringing me this far. Someday, all the pain will be useful. It has been and continues to be a long journey to get to where I ultimately hope to be, but there is no question about how much more quickly I am arriving by choosing to use my own feet to carry me.

TWENTY

-Sanctuary13-

"The love that really sets you free is the love that you decide to be."
~ Elijah Ray

{Nearly two hours away from home, I received a phone call one evening letting me know that six of you had gone through a weak place in the fence and were nowhere to be seen. I rushed home and made it back just before sunset, but it was dark before I could follow your tracks very far. All signs of you were cold, and you could have been anywhere by now. I wandered through the wilderness near our home, in the dark, desperately hoping to find you.

After sitting up most of the night, resolved to wait until the sun could aid my search, I set out to find you at dawn's first light. I walked through rugged wilderness, following every hoof print and scattered piece of manure. You guys were moving fast, and I had no idea where you might have gone. When the tracks met the highway, my heart sank low in my chest. All of the possibilities rushed through my mind, but I kept walking, tracking your every step. I finally caught up to you three miles later, all six of you together in a pasture bordering the old cattle trail that would lead us back home. I had only a single piece of rope with me. It was time to put our new relationships to the test.

I placed the rope around Harmony's neck, and I opened the gate. One by one, all six of you walked with me the entire three miles back. You could have left and run in any direction you chose, but you didn't. You stayed with me right up until we got near the front gate when you ran back inside and joined the rest of your friends. A single piece of rope. That's all it took to bring six horses home through three miles of open wilderness. That's all it took because I had earned your trust, and you knew you were free.}

+++++++++++++

In July of 2013, we left Texas and moved to Northern California with our 13 horses, just to land in Section 13 of our new subdivision, specifically on lot #13. We weren't sure what to call our new home, and one day, while I was really trying to decide, we went to a local mineral springs, and I was placed in Room 13. I finally got the message, and Sanctuary13 was born.

In the Tarot cards, number 13 is the Death Card, as in death to old ways, transformation, clearance, and change. Shai was our 13th horse. Later, when we eventually sold our home in Texas, officially closing that huge chapter of our lives, we found out that it too was on lot #13 of its subdivision. As if we needed more, the vehicle we left Texas in was our 2013 Toyota 4Runner. It seemed to be a powerful number in our lives.

At the time of this writing, Sanctuary13 is not an official organization of any kind. So far, it is simply our home, a personal sanctuary for us and the horses and other animals who live here and a place to focus on healing, growth, and transformation Our dream is to eventually open our doors to others who may wish to come here for the same things and to spend time with our horses in an unconditional way. We would like to create a foundation to support the horses and protect them for the rest of their lives. The few who have been here have all given the same confirmation that there is much to be gained by spending time with this group of animals and that they are indeed different, and we wish to share that experience with others. It would be a dream come true to teach others, especially professionals currently in the horse and therapy realms, what we have learned and how to implement change. It is our hope that, as we move forward in our lives and recover from so much change and unraveling in such a short period of time, the circumstances and support to create our vision will arrive so we can do just that.

For now, I spend my days caring for the animals and learning how to live a life much different from the one I left behind. My morning usually begins by taking the dogs out to potty, because of course all five of them think they need to sleep with me inside the tiny 19-foot travel trailer I currently call home. While they are taking care of their business, I walk over to the vintage PanAm travel trailer that was on the property when we purchased it. There is a toilet inside connected to the septic tank, but I have to bring in a bucket of water to flush it because it doesn't have any working plumbing yet. I then go back out to walk the dogs, feed them afterward, and then move on to the pig pen. Just thinking about the pigs brings a smile to my face. I am always met with the most amazing variety of noises from those silly boys. Their feelings are soulfully expressed through the tone and energy of their squeaks and snorts. Cleaning their pen comes first so that I can make sure they each get a little bit of individual attention, and then I move on to feeding and giving them fresh water. Then, I usually take a little break for myself to read and have a warm cup of lemon water with a splash of apple cider vinegar.

On most days, I force myself to go spend at least 20 dedicated minutes of being present with the horses. This is my own personal meditation for the day. Sometimes I avoid it for whatever reason, but on the days I make it happen, I always feel so much better. Things are far from the way I would like them to be out here, but walking away from your source of income so you can write a book and change your life has its own set of consequences. Everything here is a work in progress as we build a new life and put ourselves back together after a shattered reality. The animals have been super patient, giving up a lot of the things they were used to back in Texas, but we'll get there again, and it will be even better.

The horses are hand-delivered at least 400 pounds of hay each and every day. Somehow we always manage to have enough even though money is tighter than it has ever been. Something always comes through to make sure everyone has enough to eat. Once everyone is fed, I take a long look at all that is waiting to be done, and I select whatever tasks I feel up to for that day. Sometimes I need to get away and go on an adventure in nature. Sometimes I look for an escape. Other times I stay home and do the hard personal work that I came out here to do, but lately, I mostly write. Each day is filled with enormous gratitude for this peaceful place we call home. With its incredible mountain views and peaceful solitude, it is a little desert paradise, and it feels like a great place to be doing this work.

Once in a while, we get a visitor who is curious about the horses and what we are doing out here. A man brought his son out one day, a troubled young man who had just come home from a mandatory drug rehabilitation center. Coco Bueno was the first to come greet him. I watched in awe as this beautiful boy interacted with one of my favorite horses in a way that was so gentle and so aware—a way that took me over fifteen years to master. And here he was doing it with an understanding as natural as anything. The horses didn't judge him for his supposed faults. They just recognized him for who he really was, and in that moment he felt loved and understood, and I watched him light up and become the person he wanted to be. I saw the potential for what could happen if these interactions were guided and structured so that they could be taken back into a person's regular day-to-day life. Here, the horses are not seen as healers but simply as healed beings holding space for another to find that healing in themselves, where it has always been. Our horses do not heal anyone. They simply model what it is to be healed, which accelerates our own healing in their calm, loving presence.

This man and his son returned a second time to be with the horses. We cooked them a delicious vegan meal, and they helped us clean up an area where eight hands were far better at cleaning than four. Again, we saw healing before our eyes, not just for the boy as he lit up and became confident enough to share his hopes and dreams and aspirations with me, but also between a son and his father as they worked together to help us take care of the horses, expecting nothing in return. Just to have a place like this where they could come to, free of all judgment, and be fully embraced and accepted wherever they were was something powerful and inspiring to them. To just be in the presence of happy and peaceful animals was comforting beyond measure. We were beginning to see our dream come to life, even if only in scattered experiences such as these.

We've had a few other visitors over the past year, and each one has walked away from the horses forever changed by their interactions with them. I've been humbled beyond my wildest imagination to see my truth realized by others. It was not an easy path to walk down, and there is still a lot of walking to do. When I see the effect these horses have on people and how willingly the horses are to share their space with new people, I know that it has all been worth it. One of our most recent visitors, a young woman from Quebec, left us with these words:

"I have discovered another world besides language…a world made with energy, gestures, and emotions. It's a world more loving and caring. Where there are no judgments or complexity. Where we can BE…one. Thank you for that!"

This is exactly what we wish for everyone to experience who comes here. Every bit of challenge has been preparing us for everything we have ever wanted, and now it is here, and it is simply time to do the work. As we continue to work on ourselves and get our lives in order, we slowly move closer and closer to creating a sanctuary model for horses based on a thorough understanding of their biological needs and supported with unconditional love—a place where horses are healed and people come to heal themselves in their calming presence. We have no idea what our future will look like. We only know that, because our horses taught us what it really means to love, love will be what we move toward, and as it's been said before—love is all you need.